Nicolas Freeling

THE VILLAGE BOOK

A
ARCADIA BOOKS
LONDON

920
FREE

Arcadia Books Ltd
15–16 Nassau Street
London WIW 7AB

www.arcadiabooks.co.uk

First published in the United Kingdom 2002
Copyright © Nicolas Freeling 2002

Nicolas Freeling has asserted his moral right to be identified as the author of
this work in accordance with the Copyright, Designs and Patents Act, 1988.

A catalogue record for this book is available from the British Library.

ISBN 1–900850–63–x

Edited, designed and typeset in FF Scala by Discript, London WC2N 4BN
Printed in the United Kingdom by Bell & Bain Limited, Glasgow

Arcadia Books distributors are as follows:

in the UK and elsewhere in Europe:
Turnaround Publishers Services
Unit 3, Olympia Trading Estate
Coburg Road
London N22 6TZ

in the USA and Canada:
Consortium Book Sales and Distribution, Inc.
1045 Westgate Drive
St Paul, MN 55114–1065

in Australia:
Tower Books
PO Box 213
Brookvale, NSW 2100

in New Zealand:
Addenda
Box 78224
Grey Lynn
Auckland

INTRODUCTION

O NE WILL SEE AN ANT sometimes, by itself, marching fast, busy and purposeful in what is certainly the wrong direction. Children amuse themselves by planting obstacles of every nature in front of it. Stopping occasionally to consider, it will climb on undeterred, indifferent to getting nowhere. The children, bored, will look for something else to do.

As a child I was fascinated by the phrase 'the arches of the years'. I only saw one arch, for a year to a child is immense. It was a gothic arch, of clean stone, intact, standing by itself among ruins: I had probably seen a picture, striking the imagination, of some monastery destroyed by vandal soldiery. The ant set itself to climb this; would it reach the top? Perhaps, reaching the capital of the smooth pillar, after a short rest it would set out refreshed upon the bow of the arch; at the summit – what is there to do at a summit? Go on down the other side. It would have been simpler, a lot shorter, and wasted much less energy to have travelled straight across, but that doesn't occur to ants. The arches of my years have often been like this and I can sympathize with the beast.

Consider this house: bought nigh forty years ago for the children – space and fresh air after a week in cramped flats. They are all grown up and have homes of their own. We are still here. We have often moved away, and stayed away for a year on end – and returned; this house and this village mean nothing to them but has come to mean a great deal to me. Not so long ago, deciding that I had become lazy as well as self-indulgent, we made up our minds to the break and I was struck down in mid stride by an illness possibly mortal, ex-

actly like a footballer foully tackled from behind: most unfair.
I have had to stay as I am, subject to the frowns or smiles of
a lot of doctors. I am much like that ant; time and space
have played odd jokes. I began this book without knowing
where it would lead. Fiction offers similar difficulties; the
writer assembles characters, is disconcerted when they begin
to think and to do things he had not planned. There is a
'within' as well as a 'without' to a book. One can read, and
with great pleasure, a book admirably plotted in every detail,
and reach the end with disappointment; the characters have
never come to life, drilled as they are in a mechanical ordi-
nance.

Proust-like – a term to use with humility – a life treads
paths at variance to one another. His Méséglise Way becomes
a signpost towards tracing physical wanderings; obscure zig-
zags these often were. The Guermantes Way seemed to point
to the steps in a writer's world, each book a stumbling and
uncertain movement but the hope of getting further was always there.

The book thus began, for this at least was solid ground, in
and about the village.

My childhood came crowding in, as it does to all old men;
we lie in bed and remember, with an extraordinary vivacity,
in a minute ant-detail. Parentage belonged here, and the per-
plexing enigma of heredity. How much weight can we give
the tyrannical genes we carry within us? What share has the
background of our upbringing? At what point can it be said
that we exercise free will? Arbitrary, the law decides when
and where we accept responsibility, and must answer for our
actions. Indeed this has been the theme of my work, the
thread running through every book I have written. Through
irresponsibility we have all of us been criminals, if not always
with criminal intent. Occasionally we may be called to account, before the law's tribunal. Since justice is a philosophic
fiction, and jurisprudence at best a hair-splitting business, we
can sometimes get the charges reduced. I am a passionate,

and loquacious, advocate on my own behalf. And as we all know, our impulses will depend upon what we used to call pounds, shillings and pence. But in philosophy there is no avoidance. Even during our lives actions edulcorated and even effaced by the law have a way of demanding to be paid for.

For a long time – I do not know the origin of the belief – we have cherished a superstition that the lines of our life are written on the palm of the hand. Perhaps, refining this be-lief, that the within and the without could be found im-printed upon the dexter and the sinister. The idea makes an attractive illustration and a now-forgotten writer (but famous in his day: he was Osbert Sitwell) set his handprints upon the endpapers of his volumes of autobiography. A pleasant notion, thus to place his sign manual upon what he had written. This, he says, is my book and none other.

And for this one I must take responsibility.

Grandfontaine, February 2001

PART ONE

I

'THE TALE OF ANNE D.'

IT IS HARD TO LIGHT UPON the right heading. 'The Story' has an arch and even false ring to it, as though much of what follows were fabricated. This is not fiction: it is the truth. But I could not title it 'The Case' for that would imply facts seen and known, dispassionately observed. Much of this concerns a time before I was born, which I could not have witnessed. I have her word, but did she embellish? Did she even sometimes imagine? I am a fiction writer; I have been known to imagine, with power enough to confuse facts, with the conviction that my truths were factual. This history is the truth, as far as is known to me. 'A history' then? No, for this is narrowed, personal, of necessity excluding too much of the fabric from which a history is woven. And covering a longish life, it is both more and less than 'A Portrait'. 'The Tale' I think it will have to be. The Beatrix Potter smack to that is not inappropriate. Towards the end, wrapped in 'my red shawl', glasses pushed down her nose, she did often come to look like Mrs Tiggywinkle.

It could too have been called 'Romance' for much of the interest is in the fatally romantic temperament of this character; always the outstanding feature of a vivid and attractive personality.

Speaking for myself (I too come into this tale) I am not the witness – I said, and now underline – to the whole of the twentieth century. I missed nigh on thirty years of it. The year 1927 was notable for a good port vintage. But my parents were pure-juice Edwardians and my upbringing was such that the early years of the century have remained intensely alive. To few people now remaining would 'the Somme' or 'Gallipoli' mean more than the 1939–45 years of war. I make the point, since this woman's formative years were those of the first quarter of this century.

Anne Davidson was born, the middle of three children and the only girl, in 1894, into a most respectable Victorian family. Her parentage, and her ancestry, meant a great deal to her. As indeed they do to me. As indeed, it is worth noticing, to both her brothers. Both wrote memoirs, the elder's unpublished (too dull, pompous, self-centred). The younger, Michael Davidson, man of much talent, wrote a delightful book, wittily entitled *The World, the Flesh and Myself* which was – deservedly – published, but it is mostly about his own homosexuality and has little bearing on my theme. Anne wrote no memoir, although she was an accomplished writer and published four works of fiction. Well, I have done my best to fill this gap. Mike, whom I much loved, left some clues.

Their father, Walter Burn-Murdock Davidson, was of Scotch bourgeois forebears, sounding impossibly dull. There is a long row of Indian Army generals (Mike, sardonic, said he didn't believe a one of them had ever seen a shot fired in anger). Walter though was anything but a dull man. He was a mining engineer, carting about all over the world scratching up rare or sought-after minerals. A very Victorian figure; in Alaska or Patagonia, climbing Swiss glaciers or Himalayan foothills, tweed jackets and hobnailed boots, there they were, empire-building. That Walter was an interesting, valuable and sensitive man is I think beyond question. He took my grandmother on honeymoon to Japan, then barely discovered, whose civilization, painting, and poetry was just beginning to make impact upon the Western world. All her life she treasured this, as well she might: tea-ceremonies and silk robes, cherry blossom and fishing at night with paper lanterns. This story ends badly, but I must pause a moment upon my grandmother's family. For she was a 'lady', from a grand English family.

The Childers owned swathes of Yorkshire; their horses

were famous on the Doncaster racecourse. This kind of family is too grand to be Lords, while acknowledging Beauforts or Beauchamps as cousins, since they are descended (in the grander female line) from William the Norman. There exists still a genealogy, copied out lovingly in a neat schoolgirl hand. Royalty down to John of Gaunt (not perhaps an ancestor to be all that proud of) and branching thereafter into obscure but splendid byways of the English countryside, stimulating to any child of imagination. The impression is that in recent years they'd got rather dull: Hugh Culling Eardley Childers had been a minister of no great distinction in various Gladstone administrations. There was then a distinctly black-sheep episode in Ireland. Anne – romantic child – was proud of her cousin Erskine, and this would have far reaching consequences. The eldest son was always named Eardley, and so was her elder brother. Up in Yorkshire there was still a formidable old lady known as Great-Aunt Rolanda, of whom I know nothing. Clare Mostyn Childers was unmistakeably a great lady.

Perhaps it was felt that marrying a Scotch mining engineer lowered her in the social scale, but by Victorian times there was nothing untoward about this. A large armoury of sisters had done likewise and lived in large dull London houses as in *The Forsyte Saga*. Beatrice married Forbes Woodhouse, a wine-merchant famous for Madeira, and Maud married Uncle Alan, a solicitor who achieved brief fame through throwing himself under a Tube train passing Down Street: it was said because he could stand Maud's tongue no longer.

The Freelings were a lot more rackety, much more recent, and more interesting. Francis, the first, appears in England only in the early nineteenth century, and nobody knows where he came from. There are two slight clues, and perhaps they fit together. One is that there are no other Freelings in England, whereas the name is found, in Germanic variants, in Belgium, Holland and Northern Germany: Vrielings in Friesland are even quite frequent. The other is that Francis was a great crony of the Prince Regent. As is well known, Prinny was quite convinced that as a young man he had been present upon the field of Waterloo: I have wondered whether Francis was not responsible for this delusion. There were of course Dutch and German troops upon the field; might he have formed a connexion and come to England in the wake?

Whatever the truth, Francis did well for himself. The Regent showed him friendship, made him a baronet and gave him the sinecure of the Post Office (where he was the nominal chief of Anthony Trollope). The Freelings seem thus nicely launched upon fame and fortune, in which they typically show no interest. One baronet after another, seven in all and in one century, went off, sparking brightly if eccentrically, to every imaginable corner of the world, where they lost no time in dying of drink.

I have come across their traces – through letters, phone calls, amused and curious – in Australia and South Africa, in Toronto and the West Indies. The cousins. All spoke of unvarying characteristics; talent, great charm and the addiction to red wine. Taken together with this unrelenting vagabondage, the fierce pursuit of – of what exactly? – did they know? – the genetic strain is plain, persistent. One, in Spain, had taken pains, being a woman, to gather together many of these tangled threads. She died, alas, before I could meet her.

Along their brief road, for they never stayed in England long, one of these, I believe the fourth baronet, for I have still his portrait, married a Childers girl.

By the end of the nineteenth century, when Anne was born, the head of such Freelings as remained was a splendid old lady of eccentric nature, permanently flown on claret, Aunt Annie. As children Anne and her brothers went often to stay with her. She claimed the little girl as a 'true Freeling' in whom this strange restless blood ran unadulterated. It is a pity that the rule of primogeniture obliged her to will a considerable collection of family souvenirs to Eardley, who (true

Davidson) promptly sold the lot. Anne inherited nothing but the blood, which, for such are the jokes of genetics, she would presently pass to her own son.

I must gather now these threads together, assemble them in 1894 and remark that practically from the day of her birth the little girl, Anne Freeling Davidson, was always and throughout her life called Nancy. I have still some of her books; the beloved Kiplings bought as they came out, signed on the flyleaf 'N.F.D.' in a handwriting already recognizably mature. But it is time to look at the earliest, and perhaps the longest-lasting tragedy in her life.

Walter, her father, in his wanderings around the world, contracted the Victorian disease. That it was syphilis I have no doubt at all: he became largely paralysed and intermittently insane. Nancy's loyalty maintained always a polite fiction, the invention of Victorian doctors, entitled 'Jacksonian epilepsy'. She must have known the truth; it can be deduced from her immense love for her father combined with her lifelong shrinking from sexual relations, found first difficult, then dreaded and finally banished totally: this would become the salient feature of all her many love affairs, that they had all to be sublimated into impossible Platonic ideals.

Certainly Clare knew; she moved her helpless man to a pretty house by the seaside, in Guernsey, away from inquisitive eyes and clacking tongues: here the children passed early and largely happy years.

It is a moralistic picture, such as the Victorians loved: the man laid low, nursed by a devoted valet; his one joy a toy Yorkshire terrier – and the bright, delightful, talkative small daughter. Flowers grew at the open window. He could hear and smell the sea.

Kipling's magnificent story, 'Love o' Women', belongs in this context: here she first read it and this too was never forgotten.

His widow moved back to a pleasant country cottage in Hampshire, where she had an aviary of singing birds. The boys went to Lancing, a school of immense pious respectability. Nancy to an establishment for young ladies in Seaford, and to a finishing-school in Paris, where the romantic girl discovered Rodin and Rostand; the beautiful gas-lit Paris and the exquisite Ile-de-France: loves that would be lifelong. There was a passionate friendship with a girl called Jim. Nothing physical; she was not in the least lesbian. Her tragedy would be that men found her intensely attractive, and she them. She was never pretty. Shortish and if anything dumpy. 'I had pretty feet.' Slim then, springy, filled with vitality. Good skin, fine grey eyes, the hair bobbed in the manner of the time (and never changed), a boyish athletic look; she loved to ride and to swim.

London next, the nominal, one may guess casual chaperonage of Aunt Maud. Young girls had to *be presented*, make their curtsey, have their season, go to dances, meet eligible young men. None of this interested her in the slightest. Nothing could be more boring than this staid, stuffy world. Her intellect was sharp and already formed. Always impatient, she was greedy for intellectual pleasures. In passing, I know nothing of her father's family, but a cousin was introduced as an eminently suitable match; Dick Davidson was worthy, steady, making his way in the world. 'Poor Dick' I would hear thirty years later. 'I could never marry him – so very dull.' The world in which she found herself happy is well documented, and from the fragmentary allusions of this sort can be pieced together.

Intellectual excitement. London was full of the famous Cambridge dynasties; the Darwins, Stracheys, Huxleys. Two young, brilliant, pretty girls, of much the same type, were keeping house for their father, Sir Leslie Stephen. She seem to have liked neither Virginia nor Vanessa. Perhaps she was right: in retrospect both were overestimated. But Bertie Russell's 'Dora' has much in common with the Nancy of these years. The 'girls of the 1917 Club', celebrated in so many of the 1920s jokes – many of these were fellow-travellers. The word is chosen deliberately, for of course she became a Communist. I must of necessity telescope these years. The intellectual ferment can be dated roughly from about 1912, the eager girl of eighteen in the Edwardian hey-day, and the middle 1920s when the great crash of her life took place. I must attempt to trace the character as it devel-oped. Medical students, budding poets and painters (she never understood either), students of economics (of which she knew nothing). There was a fervent lover, called of course Walter. There was no limit to this new wild world.

Yes, there was. She never became a true 'Bloomsbury' en-thusiast. They were not sufficiently fastidious. Or was she too prudish? Virginia and Vanessa stripped naked at parties; there was a good deal of sleeping with one another's men. This was not good enough. Idealisms burned fiercely: one might and did strip naked to bathe but the prurient eye or hand meant instant banishment. I am quite certain that she was a virgin at marriage. Even among the boys this austerity was widely shared.

Fiction so often illuminates detail that history obscures. *Cold Comfort Farm* is with much wholesome mockery a good guide. Flora Poste is not like Nancy, being cool, detached and self-possessed; she 'cannot abide a mess'. She goes for a walk with Mr Mybug, an acid portrait of the sub-Bloomsbury circle, who is impressed by the chestnut buds – god, what an urgent, phallic look! Flora fails to respond to this well-worn gambit. They were all of course writing fearful books (Mr Mybug, typically, about Branwell Brontë). The budding au-thoress was also making herself felt; quite a lot about clean-limbed young men naked in pools (so was Rupert Brooke). They were not all homosexual, but in this at least resembling Flora, Nancy was fastidious.

Cambridge was a magnet: here one found pure souls. A parenthesis here, of some importance. She was oddly defi-cient in the aesthetic tastes of the time. Knowing nothing about painting might be in reaction against people she did not care for, like Carrington or Vanessa Bell, but to music she was also insensitive. I cannot to this day make sense of her marrying a musician.

In the grove of Academe 'old Doctor Southward' was a landmark, Master of Saint Cath's; a charming old gentleman with a son, Chris, said – I really do not know because neither did she – to be a musician of talent. The only light to be found is from a novel of many years later – *The Pursuit of Love*. The delightful Linda marries a pompous bore: why? There isn't any answer; girls did, and do. Nancy's subsequent accounts do certainly 'Poor Chris' less than justice. A party piece was that on honeymoon in some fishing port where the speciality was tiny, delicious, fresh-caught lobsters, Chris was said to have demanded shepherd's pie. But apart from claiming that boredom was insufferable, she always turned vague and became evasive, much like Linda or indeed Miss Mitford who married Peter Rodd . . .

To this marriage a daughter was born in 1916, another in 1918. The war seems to have touched her little. Both her brothers served, as young regimental officers, and both survived. One has I think some natural distaste for the many excuses, not always admirable, found by Bloomsbury in avoidance of all service. Warfare is detestable. One may hate; one may fear. I shall have occasion to touch again upon this point, after following Nancy up to 1939. Some of her friends were conscientious objectors and went to Dartmoor on that account: some volunteered for stretcher-bearing and the like. I do not know what Chris did, or thought.

Wartime or not, the wedding was splendid. There exists a studio photograph, no doubt much touched up, but Nancy in her satin and lace is grave, erect, almost beautiful, and dare I say touching? I have no doubt that she did her best and that so did Chris. The fault would lie on neither side. Marriage under Victorian auspices was no sinecure. She was sure to be a bolter, but that is not altogether a blameable characteristic. The overstrained nervous horse is not on that account a worthless horse. Equally, one cannot complain of wanting to get rid of it.

The young couple were comfortably off. A largish and pleasant country house, not very far from Cambridge, was theirs. Since, today, people find it very difficult to imagine this kind of living, I may choose – to illuminate – the detail of servants.

This was not a large house. There would be no butler nor footmen. The reception rooms were the parlourmaid's province. A smart and rather elegant young woman – well, youngish, and if possible, pretty. With nice manners, who said 'Madam' and was of superior sort. Even then it was difficult to get good ones, properly trained, and especially in the country. She opened the door to people and knew how to handle every category of guest. She served at table, polished the furniture and the silver, and helped you on with your coat. She was black-dressed, white-aproned, and might even be silk-stockinged and high-heeled – personable. She also had heavy manual work; she polished the floor on her knees, brought coal-scuttles: the fires on this floor were part of her duty. In a wealthy household she might have had a hall-boy or page to help with the heaviest work.

Upstairs was a housemaid, probably elderly and with no special dress. She made beds, brought hot water, looked after the fires on this floor, kept everything fresh and bright, was responsible for linen, did much of the washing and most of the ironing, sewed, mended and was always on the trot. The young, newly-married lady – Nancy – did not often have a personal lady's-maid. She had been trained (my grandmother was strict on the subject) to fend for herself, to ask nothing of servants she could not herself do. She had been carefully brought-up, dressed herself, did her own intimate laundry, was handy with a needle and thread, was expected to know, and thoroughly, every detail of household management. Only the 'new rich' were helpless. A 'lady' had the respect of her servants; she could and did lend a useful hand to anything needful, and thought nothing of climbing on a step-ladder to take down the curtains for cleaning. A nursery-maid, generally a young country girl, looked after the children, fed, washed and dressed them, played with them and exacted a roughish discipline. The bringing-up, the training and education of little ones, was the mother's job. Nancy would not have dreamed of having a nanny (ignorant women, putting everything unsuitable in a child's head). Her ideas of child care, of medicine, of hygiene, of psychology, were Victorian (not much the worse, for that). She thought herself a thoroughly modern young woman; free; emancipated. The same illusion prevails today.

There would be a cook of course, in the vast sombre basement. A lady could also cook, knowledge of the subject being indispensable to good household management, but the cooks of these days were tyrannical, brooked no interference and were best left alone. Since she was kind-hearted and considerate Nancy was liked by her servants, but she was never conspicuous for tact. Outside there would be a gardener, and conceivably a boy. Flower- and kitchen-garden, orchard and paddock. Horses were still very much an indispensable fact of country existence: it is probable that there were stables. She was never known to have a car; bicycled I think, enthusiastically. Perhaps a pony-trap for the children. Loved her horse (called of course Rosinante) and rode much. There is a photograph in riding breeches, which suited the boyish style. The railway network of the time was dense and efficient: one took a local train into Cambridge or to wherever one might wish; an express to London. I do not know exactly where this house lay.

There exists a painting, in a typical Bloomsbury style; stiff and oily, as though from the brush of Vanessa or Mark Gertler. Nancy is in the nursery (in the background is a large expensive rocking-horse) reading aloud to the children; seated on a throne in a loose flowing robe; the girls on each side, picturesquely dressed (dark blue velvet with a lace collar, the little one in orange, with long hair; the robe is grey).

The painting has no merit, would now have an antiquarian interest, the stiff composition being the perfect juice of the time. 'Poor Chris' is nowhere to be seen, nor felt.

I know nothing of this house: it all went in the crash, as though bombed flat, and not a lot survived save, typically, books. Twenty years later, counting on our fingers, it was worked out that during that time alone she had moved house eight times. Some of the books were still there. And many more than eight times later, after eighty years (another Freeling has succeeded to the task) still are.

What follows touches myself closely but I have never known the whole of the truth. There are reticences which must be respected. The modern biographer tears away layers of personal history long buried. A healthy and brutal hand, as though he were peeling onions. Old scars are exposed, and perhaps unhealed ulcers beneath a thin protective membrane. Even if there is no witness left alive, no documentation. Papers – letters, diaries? – but no; all gone. It is just as well: one might have been tempted. Much, and most of it, sad and painful, can be pierced together. None can be guessed at. Rooting about in psychology has dangers, even for the professional. Discretion is easier when one does not know. One may prefer not to know. What is known; those few facts which are certain; these can be set down, unadorned and also unprotected.

Norfolk lies not far from Cambridge. An example of involuntary discretion, a reticence born of psychological pressures barely guessed at, is that I have never been there. Playing one day with the child, my father wrote a word joke.

> 'Which witch for Ipswich?'
> 'No witch – gone to Norwich.'

I have never set foot in either. Why do I remember?

The children of this very English county incline to be more English than most. Snobberies exist about 'those Germans at Sandringham'. Nelson, famous son of Norfolk, felt very strongly about patriotism and got very heated when he thought of the French. There exists here an arrangement which may be known elsewhere but was here frequent; the local squire was also the Rector. Of such a family, a younger son among numerous boys and at least one girl, Walter – yes, another Walter – was born in I think 1888 or -9. I am unsure even of the date and have no idea of the parish. It would have been quite easy to find out, and I am now unhappy that I never did. It is enough at present to say that this was a country boy, growing up in good farming land. He loved and was good at country pursuits, skilled with a gun and a dry fly. Son of the manse which was also the manor, he can be classified as a small country gentleman, a category well-known and instantly recognizable in the England of up to 1939, which was also the year of his death. If asked to particularize, say from personal appearances, I might say that he carried his watch in a waistcoat pocket. This watch was of gun-metal, as befitted gentlemen, and was fastened with a leather bootlace: he spoke also of his 'boots', not of his shoes. (His turns of speech were characteristic.)

Norfolk sons of good family did not go to Eton, or the three or four establishments of this ilk. They were sent to an equally ancient and locally-famous foundation – Gresham's School Holt. The head of this seat of learning, famous at Headmasters' Conferences for his Honour System, was Mr Howson, who occupies a place in the history of English pedagogy nigh as resounding in Victorian annals as Dr Arnold of Rugby. Mr Howson's System was this (today's education psychologist blanches even to his hair): no boy lied, cheated, stole, masturbated, otherwise failed to reach the ideal, without honourably coming to his housemaster to confess and make amends. Other boys might wallow in moral turpitude: a Holt boy never. I suppose one might say 'hardly ever' – Hugh Auden and Ben Britten were both Holt boys. Walter, God help him, was in the School House, presided by Mr H. in person; became Head of House, Captain of the School, apple of the fearful old gentleman's eye. It's pretty plain that a perverted sense of honour would be a lifelong tare: one will always be on the verge of failure.

It is all in the bound volumes, stamped with the Gresham arms, of the school magazine. Here is Walter captaining the rugby team, a full-back judicious in defence and daring in counter-attack; cricket captain in summer (stylish bat, useful change bowler, at cover-point a joy to watch); outstanding at athletics (victor ludorum), gymnastics, swimming. How the little boys must have worshipped. A Kipling reader would say 'Good God, it's the Brushwood Boy' and perhaps Nancy did. I feel it all with pain, for his son inherited no trace of these talents.

School magazines being what they are, there is not much to be learned about more intellectual endeavours. He seems to have been an average student. Mr Howson's blue-eyed boy would in any case have a safe passport to King's College Cambridge.

Here – I hate thinking of this – a second and more dreadful trauma waited. Victorian notions of virtue were toxic; how much more so, to a boy of these physical gifts, the dread Victorian illness called rheumatic fever. The muscles of the heart, pronounced the medical faculty, were gravely, indeed fatally impaired. If the subject of this clinical judgement were to be very careful indeed, in monastic avoidance of all strenuous activity, he might have an expectancy of a few years. Snip: the Parcae.[1] Told to a boy of twenty. No Double Blue; and if a life, then what life? A pass degree in biology would get him an usher's job. Was there any help offered? The Rector appears to have been a selfish and brutal man: I have never heard a word about his mother. I have his statement that he found his brothers unsympathetic. The one close to him, Reggie, was killed in the trenches of Flanders; in the thinking of the time a heroic end, and one

---

1. The Parcae are the Fates, who spin man's life-thread. Best known is Atropos who cuts the thread with her scissors – 'Snip'.

not allowed to himself. It is at this moment that the comet Nancy appears upon a scene which must have been very narrow, and have appeared very bleak.

What happened? I cannot believe in any flaming love affair, in the conjunction of two stars. Taking pity upon this lame duck? – more than that. It can only be guesswork. Of her devotion to her father there is no doubt. There is the coincidence of name, of a terrible illness thought shortly to be fatal, and there may have been some likeness physically, of voice or manner. Here was a young woman, amusing and attractive, of great gaiety and vitality, whose house was open to a cluster of Cambridge Young-Woodleys.[2] It would be natural that he should fall head over heels, but what could have impelled her to bolt? Chris was a bore; it is not enough. No one every spoke of it. Her mother must have known, and she did not withdraw love and loyalty. Others may have known: there were friends who remained constant all her life. But to bolt meant a terrible smash; first of all, a comfortable household.

'Oh dear; I had such a pretty dinner set. Bow, with every plate painted with different lovely flowers. Auctioneers, dear, see to it that whatever one has it all goes for three ha'pence.'

Bolting meant exile. This is pure Dickens; Mr Alfred Lammle gets into difficulties and the result is Boulogne; it is never questioned that this is inevitable, and there were many such. There were other inducements, of economic nature: in the years following the War the pound bought a lot of francs and colonies of English living on small fixed invested income settled in pleasant French towns. Pau was one such, and Dinard was another. Characteristically Nancy settled 'somewhere odd'. Le Croisic is a tiny fishing village on the outermost Atlantic of Brittany. In 1925 a romantic place. When the sun sinks into the sea and the twilight grows, the gulls cry mournfully, and the lighthouses of a dangerous coast answer one another with their message of safety and security,

---

2. In a play famous between the wars, young Woodley was a schoolboy who fell in love with his housemaster's wife.

then it is easy to imagine the ship bringing Isolde to Tristan.

Here Walter found peace of a sort. He learned to fish, off the rocky point. He learned to paint, humble, careful; showing, once basic techniques learned, a good sense of composition. Conventional subjects; the sardine boats in harbour, the pyramids of salt after evaporation in the tiny pans fed at high water. Lessons in light and in colour; very English these gentle, quite accomplished sea- and skyscapes. But the restless woman was not long in complicating existence. The Communist made the decision to turn Catholic. This quite frequent impulse is always explosive.

She forced upon Walter a horrible bargain; one would say ignoble but for having the distorted, crippled nobility which often will illuminate the impulse to such concepts. The *Morte d'Arthur* was among her favourite books, and she always indulged herself in romantic legend. It was laid down that she would sleep with him until a child was born. Should this child be a boy – a promise, a *sign* – they would thereafter live as brother and sister. She saw always her life in these terms; some splendid renunciation and an entry into heaven like that in *A Tale of Two Cities* (another of her favourites). The sadness, the silliness, never occurred to her. When she found herself pregnant the die was cast. One can only suppose that Walter was so dependent upon her as to accept: his dreadful sense of Honour would force him to keep to it.

Nancy's final Communist fling would be typically theatrical. Her child would be born in London, and 'properly'. No padded bourgeois clinic would do for the accomplishment of the *Sign*; no vulgar Wimpole-Street gynaecologist would pollute fulfilment. No, the birth must be on the ward. Thus, in the heart of Bloomsbury – the Royal Free Hospital in the Gray's Inn Road. 'Queen Mary came to see you when you were born.' Amused since nobody was less of a snob. Certainly, for it was the Queen Mary Ward, and royalty showing the habitual kindly patronage towards the poor. The good woman was no doubt taken aback to hear a cosy, comforting question answered in the confident ringing upper-class voice I can still hear.

There: I have got myself born. The beginnings of many things traumatic, but most of them, at least in retrospect, comic.

2

SPEAK MEMORY

BLOOMSBURY RALLIED ROUND. Many an ex-lover fussed about. I cringe because it is so pure-juice: the news was spread on little postcards with Handel's musical notation to the words of 'Unto us a child is given'. Oh dear! – and not for the last time. Prideful, she carried her baby back to Le Croisic. I would remember this, finding ourselves on the Saint-Malo boat thirty years after with our own first son in a basket; French girl students crowding sentimentally around saying '*Oh, quel mignon*'.

Another trauma, only three months later, when a picnic on the beach was decided and various foodstuffs were crammed into the baby's pram, among them a thermos full of nice boiling-hot tea. Alack, thermos faulty, baby set up a horrible yell, but it took some minutes to discover and unwind a badly burned small child. I carry to this day a massive scar from hip to foot, but the trauma was hers for it was extremely doubtful whether the baby would live. A patient old country doctor would (with perseverance, devotion, calm and common sense) save it. Hence a lifelong conviction, not unjustified, that 'only French doctors are any good'.

She had been badly frightened: the *sign* might get taken away. The episode is mentioned because it was the start of another obsession: that this was a highly delicate child. So it was, though accident-prone might be more accurate, but surrounding its every moment with precautions and medicaments is no way to handle a fragile nervous child. One will not sit its bare bottom on the stoop to harden it, but a bit of healthy neglect is salutary. Recalling that Nancy slept with this child in the night nursery until it was past twelve years old one will be surprised that it could ever behave normally.

Perhaps the balancing element is farce – where she was concerned, never far off.

The first example is found at the child's christening: many children are saddled with farcical names but few are this preposterous. 'Diamond' comes from a Victorian book; it is a little boy, and is also a horse. Many years later I found a small enjoyment in titling a book *At the Back of the North Wind* and was gleeful when a reviewer, so often both arrogant and silly, declared that I had plainly never heard of George Macdonald. 'Arthur' is a perfectly good name, but I have mentioned her tiresome preoccupation with this legendary hero. But 'Sigurd' is hard to forgive: yet another Victorian book – William Morris's tedious retelling in humdrum verse of the Siegfried legend. Placing these three names cumulatively, in all seriousness, shows an amazing insensitivity. It took the child years to shake off.

And yet she did not lack a sense of farce. An anecdote belonging to this time became a notable party piece. Even in reduced circs they kept some bourgeois features of life-style, like servants: Jeanne, the *bonne*, and her husband Maurice, gardener–handyman. It was remembered that he in a previous existence had been a notable cook, and that she knew how to wait at table. Nancy and Walter decided to give a dinner-party and to invite district notables like the *sous-préfet*. This was a great success. Remnants of silver were polished; Maurice in cook's whites and Jeanne in parlourmaid's black achieved a notable formal meal. The farce – a very French farce – was not long in arriving. Every guest – four or five couples – felt obliged to return the compliment and did. In the subsequent months 'the English' ate the identical menu four more times. It got harder and harder to suppress the *fou-rire*, French for ungovernable giggles. It was very rare, even at home, for Walter not to be a gentleman. At home, Nancy was never a lady but in the houses of others I never knew her forget the manners of her upbringing, and being a 'lady' remained an essential and even striking feature of her personality.

Another move was called for. This must have been linked to the irresistible rush now gathering impetus towards the Catholic faith. It is a truism that ex-Communists make the most fervent and even the most fanatical of converts. Northern Brittany was (to some extent still is) a place of solid – indeed reactionary – religious faith; swarmed with nuns, processions, and improbable local saints. Saint-Servan lies just outside the old walled town of Saint-Malo, in my recollections a grey and gloomy little place made vivid by two remarkable friends. Louise Vincent was a sculptress of some talent who abandoned a promising career in Paris to devote herself to aged, ailing and distinctly trying parents. Her Catholicism was of the saintly character and one does not say that in joke. Yvan Vincent, delightful and gifted man, had left behind a career in letters to earn his living as a journalist locally. He was a little embittered to be thus buried in this dusty provincial backwater, but had put loyalty before inclination. Both were witty, of the sharpest intelligence, and highly sophisticated. Nancy loved them deeply.

Thirty years on, Louise would find for me a perfect tiny vignette. 'We were invited to dinner. There we sat round a big bowl of nice soup, Nancy standing with one foot on her chair, conducting her orchestra with the ladle. She talked, most interestingly. She went on talking. Fascinating but I do remember thinking – Darling, do for the love of God give us something to eat.'

Nancy's other great friend was a nun, a woman of sophistication as well as sanctity, wisdom and French common sense. Her nuns, simple peasant women, walking by the seashore, found a box left by the tide. Balloons, just the job for Reverend Mother's feast day. Since they were contraceptives Elizabeth had much ado to hold back the giggles to which Nancy gave uproarious outlet. Louise, poor childless woman, was shocked by these impieties. I think that 'my darling Elizabeth' did much to deepen and enrich the fervour of Catholicism, and that she would have known how to temper the excesses of the ensuing years.

It was all too good to last. The girls were not getting the education they needed, and in England the holy nuns of 'La Sainte Union' were famous for the intellectual dimension given to forming the female adolescent. So that back we all went: Walter perturbed by the depression which in 1931 was causing havoc. In a fit of financial panic he bought a tiny house in a Southampton slum – no no, one must be accurate; Shirley was an 'honest working-class district'. A child of five does not grasp these social considerations, but can certainly see that things are wrong somewhere...

A child in the early formative years, between four and twelve. Every tiny happening thickly sown, strongly seeded. These years of the 1930s are of the greatest moment. Indelible stamps, most vividly remembered, in microscopic detail; one could fill a book and so I did, and tore it all up. I will come back, in the end, to one or two of the signposts on the long road to this village. Not now; this is Nancy's story, and I must compress these years into a few paragraphs.

The 1930s to be sure are of absorbing interest: these are the depression years which finished the century of Victorian certainties and self-sufficient vanity; which saw the Empire totter towards disintegration; which would give birth after a great war and a great social upheaval to our modern world. The years of Hitler, and of the Spanish Civil War, and of Mrs Simpson. And the decade of my childhood is *the* decade, after which everything will be anti-climax: the years of happiness and of terror, and of blinding misery, of magic and poetry, of the world without and the worlds within. There is no foretaste of the horrible decade to come.

In the Southampton years Walter plays an increasingly small part. He fades. He is there, and sometimes he makes his presence felt. But he withdrew. I must suppose that he had never expected to live this long, that he had always known the world he knew and valued would come to nothing in the end. He could see it all decaying, great lumps falling off and washing away. He was readying himself for death. Death came on cue, in 1939.

Nancy occupies centre-stage, strident and voluble, immensely active. The new religious ferment occupied her totally. Walter had not subscribed to Roman dogmas. This pushed him further into the shadows. She carried her children with her on a noisy tide of ceremonies and observances, fasts and feasts, high holidays and penitential preparations. The Church, in England, was militant and aggressive.

There are thus two salient features occupying the terrain around her. One is the houses, dottier than ever. The other became known generically as the 'Roman collars'.

The priests of France and Italy (for of 'the Continent' as it was called, and incredibly still is, these were the countries we knew) wore the soutane, the full-length robe which buttons down the front: you would go far to see one today. English priests wore suits of decent black. But all wore the starched white circlet at the neck which everywhere signalled the road to Rome.

But before they could invade the houses these must be situated and clearly seen. They are of the most vital importance to a child. As Nancy advanced in eccentricity, her immediate surroundings became ever dottier. 'Walter's Folly', Ampthill Road in Shirley, was a mean and miserable little dwelling, in a Victorian terrace which could never be anything but both, and my own memories of it are few. Save this: it opened into Foundry Lane and this was a bare step from the docks. The 1930s were the last decade of the great passenger liners, and Southampton especially was the terminus of the transatlantic routes. The child got to know them all well, loved them, and here is one of the great treasures of these years.

A house like this could not contain the riches of an abundant and exuberant personality, but even here she made friends, among working-class housewives – she never paid a ha'p'orth of heed to social barriers. But she did have to admit that it was a poky little horror, and was relieved when Walter typically bought (as ill-advisedly as possible) a suburban villa of the most flushed sort. 'Montreux', Midanbury Lane, was just as horrible as Ampthill Road – 180 degrees the other way. It was turreted, bay-windowed, tennis-courted and con-servatoried, with a large garden such as he had hankered for, and an airy prosperous situation. Out of the petty-bourgeois streets of Bitterne Park one climbed a steepish hill. This was the outskirt of the town. The main road went on, up Lance's Hill, into Bitterne village. Climb Midanbury Lane (the house next door was called Normandie...) you were in leafy coun-tryside. This was as far as one could get from Shirley. Nancy bicycled through the town to see her friends and even kept her grocer: Mr Clifford would come every week to the door to take her order. There were now no servants but the char, Mrs Gardiner, came daily, now supported by her daughter Lily.

This house, as outrageous as the other, could not endure long; at best I think two years for each. It must have been 1935 when the last of the Southampton houses brought strong magic into a child's life. A life filled with humiliation and misery, but for four golden years happiness would fill and brim over, never again to be recaptured on this earth. Our house here in this French village, a source of peace and joy many times four years, could be only the palest, thin and etiolated shadow of the world that was then my own.

Walter came quickly to realize that he was living beyond his means – eating capital, the great crime of Edwardian bourgeoisdom. Another mighty retrenchment must take place, to the most eccentric house I have ever lived in – or Nancy either.

It came about through a nigh-forgotten link with her girl-hood. Her mother, withdrawing from the sadness of Guernsey, had settled in a charming 'widow's house' called Yew Tree Cottage, not far outside Bitterne village. As was natural she knew, to some small degree she frequented the 'houses' of the neighbourhood, for Clare Childers would never have been less than a lady we know. And among these 'people one knows' were the Culme-Seymours at Bitterne Manor. I cannot but give way to some self-indulgence: I will keep this parenthesis as brief as may be, though this too is a part and an important part of 'The Tale of Anne D'. It has got the better of me.

3

Bitterne Manor House

IT LAY ENCLOSED AND SECRET within a loop of the River Itchen. Across the water, widish here and tidal as it neared the estuary, lay industrial Southampton, metallic and grimy. Upstream, Cobden Bridge linked countryside to the urban huddle of Portswood and St Denys. Downstream Northam Bridge, iron girders that swayed fascinatingly at the passage of heavy traffic, led to the centre of the town. On this side the Bitterne Park estate had been sold to developers: residential streets of petty-bourgeois comfort. Only the garden remained, large and overgrown by trees, silent and even sinister. From the road nothing could be seen: a massive stone wall and high iron gates gave privacy. A long drive was lined with woodland, frightening at night. Only when quite close one discovered the house, the front with a perspective of gravel and lawn, and beyond such flowerbeds as were still kept up. But past the stable yard and winding round to the back the drive became only a gravelled path lined with laurel, and the whole back garden down to the river had slipped to wilderness, a solitary playground for a small boy, filled with fir and ilex. The big house was not ruinous but largely abandoned: one saw the owners seldom and only in the summer. There were still two lame old gardeners.

This house was without distinction; a gaunt four-square block with two lower wings. Walter acquired the far ballroom wing for a peppercorn rent; a friendly gesture I should think, to Clare Davidson's daughter. The owners caught sight of gave a friendly smile, stopped for a polite word, but there was no intimacy. I have been in the house three or four times. High on a wall, of the hall surely, were pinned eight or ten oars with blue blades: the Culme-

Seymours were a famous rowing family.

Not a great deal of work was needed; done in pragmatic and primitive fashion. Nobody had used the ballroom in a hundred years. A back entrance gave access to a butler's pantry, turned into a little kitchen with a hatchway to our one splendid living-room. From here a passage where we kept bicycles led to the ballroom, totally empty and good only for the child to play in when it was wet. In the corner of this a lavatory had been expanded into a wooden cabin; this was the bathroom. On the window side a stairway no more than a straight ladder of plain deal steps pierced the ceiling. Up here a landing gave on two upper-servants' bedrooms; a governess perhaps and a head housemaid. There was a lovely Victorian lav with a huge mahogany seat. Here my father slept.

A few steps led upward to the nursery wing, built here so that the children should be well out of sight and sound; quite a typical arrangement. A passage led back to the centre of the house past long-unused guest bedrooms. The day nursery was long, and here Nancy had a sitting-room of her own, and in the other half her bedroom (with a bed alongside for the child...). Next door was the old night nursery, shared by the girls.

I have mentioned the one splendid room. This had been perhaps the house library. Too large and too fine for a morning-room or gun-room; square, with a magnificent window to the front and the sun.

On the kitchen side was the dining-table; a heavy curtained door in this corner led back to the house. All of that wall was bookshelves. The space here may be imagined; in the centre stood a large occasional table and in the window embrasure a writing-desk. Plenty of space remained for a living-room area, two sofas and various armchairs grouped around the only source of proper heat in the entire place: a Courtier stove in the fireplace, Walter's pride and joy. When the massive steel doors with their mica inserts were opened this made a comforting blaze. When these doors were closed, for night-time *continu* or simply on a mild but dampish day, Nancy would sit directly upon the fretted enamelled iron-work: bliss. Pulling up voluminous skirts and perching with a lavish display of woolly knickers; we were always afraid she would do this in front of guests. This room was at every moment delicious. Everywhere else of course was a shudder. English country houses are legendary. Even in the mild Hampshire climate, so close to the river, forever damp, chill, musty. The bedrooms had the wretched little gas stoves familiar to all of my generation. In winter the paraffin heaters remembered likewise, and loved by a child for the kaleidoscope pattern cast upon the ceiling.

The walls of this house were thick, the nursery windows in their deep embrasures appearing small, square, with shutters on the inside in the English fashion, folding back upon the thickness of the wall. Close them, and a little door appeared which – strictly forbidden – led to the roofs, concealed in baronial style by battlements. Little ladders allowed a workman to examine or repair (much needed) the leads. To the child it was a secret passage of the most exciting and dangerous kind, frequented by the witches.

Plainly, it was a hideous house, a bleak English barrack of the nineteenth century with ill-judged gothic embellishments. Probably (as often) it had replaced an earlier and much better building. For it was a historic site: here had stood the Roman camp of Clausentum. This fact had only recently come to light. The university archaeological people had been given permission to dig at the back, and had uncovered a massive wall of the chalky local stone full of fossils, bound with the pink, beautiful Roman cement. Our pride was that in a patch of this appeared the imprint, nail-studded and vividly fresh, of a sentry's sandal ... But digging anywhere – Walter wished for a rosebed but we were all bitten by the mania – one turned up Samian pottery, sealing-wax red and with decorations in relief, not merely incised; coins, and many bones. We found – so rich was the site – an entire skeleton intact, and a milestone – the beginnings of a road ... to where did it lead? This was all more magic, further stimulation of a child's overactive imagination. The house also had mighty cellarage, where Walter grew mushrooms, fondly imagining he might sell them at a profit.

Save perhaps in the very last year, it would be a mistake to think that he had given in altogether. Deprived of his wife, cut off from his son, embittered and miserable, he still had his intelligence, and his sensitive hands. He found astonishingly much to interest him. One can laugh at these amiable toys. His soul was not dead. I am going to list here some of his activities. For they are all I have of him. Here, in the middle of Nancy's story, and in the beginnings of my own, I must celebrate this sad unhappy man.

I see him, in the living-room at Bitterne Manor House, for this was his and not hers for once. I owe this to my children. I have little of him but he, their grandfather, gave them much. It is strongest in my second son, the countryman, hunter, Jaeger, expert in flora and fauna, and who built his own house with his own hands. Walter sits, still and silent, smoking his pipe. It is winter, and he is busied with indoor activities. With a board across his knees, covered in green baize, he is playing patience (a little book gave a hundred and twenty-five varieties). He likes cards, and has taught my younger sister chess; she became good enough to play for the university. Me he has taught bézique, the great Edwardian stand-by. And piquet – eighteenth century. Beside him is his knitting; all his socks, for turning the heel was a challenge to skill: there are also cardigans whose buttons are enamelled and jewelled; those of his long-ago evening shirts.

On the occasional table is the canvas, half-completed, of one of his hand-stitched hearthrugs. Outside in the ballroom is his carpenter's bench, the chisels ranged, oiled and razor-sharp. Up in his bedroom is the paraphernalia of his leather-work; shopping bags that could never wear out and were given as Christmas presents. And throughout the year he cooked. Nancy would never be any good. She stood in a dream, and 'Hark, the milk is boiling over'. This irritated Walter, who liked food. Very well, chemistry he also liked; he would learn to do it himself.

It started with the simple things he loved and knew from his own Norfolk childhood. Vegetable-marrow-and-ginger jam. Suet roly-poly, treacle tart. Lancashire hotpot, a Yarmouth bloater, game pie. Atavistic – jugged hare, a roast pheasant. Never-never will a butcher learn to hang them long enough. Partridges ... I do not think one finds grouse, in Norfolk. He began to remember things seen and learned purely by observation in France. Fish, shellfish. How to casserole a chicken. He made friends with Mr Minns, the Bitterne Park butcher, and quoted with relish the saying – 'It'll eat very sweet, and cut very satisfying' – English to his bones; nobody in France ever has or ever will understand 'butcher's meat'. He would cite, pleasurably, the sayings of the 'Norfolk farmer', Mr Betts. Carving the roast, as a gentleman does at his own dinner-table, Mr Betts would always lose his temper. 'Everyone eating, and me not begun yet.' But the favourite anecdote was at breakfast-time. Mrs Betts would say, 'I've a nice piece of salmon for you.' Betts, on the fields since dawn, would be enraged. 'What's a pound of salmon to a man like me? Bring four boiled eggs.' And how he loved young rhubarb. But only the French knew how to roast lamb pink, make a *daube* or cook a potato ... He was on the whole a lucky cook because he could see the blind spots of both countries while enjoying their merits.

Summer activities saw him out and about. He would put his bicycle on the train, get out at some little country station and ride gravely around the New Forest. He had a rich friend with fishing rights on the Test, the famous trout stream. He gardened in a small humble way. Many hours were spent on the riverbank with his easel and camp-stool; both bridges, again and again, cloud and tide water. Here he read aloud to the child, who learned most of Dickens this way. He liked to potter in the poor quarters of the town and bring back something violent for supper. And one day he won a smallish prize for a crossword puzzle, and spent it on a fine complete edition of Conrad. After over twenty more moves I have it still.

There are famous houses which have nothing to say to a child, such as the Doll's House or the House of Bernarda Alba. Others, in any country, in which children's magic is understood and practised – like the houses of Fanny and Alexander (few artists have had Bergman's sensitivity to childhood). My own, with which this one became woven, was Kay Harker's Seekings House. Masefield, an immensely popular writer between the wars, was not a good one in either prose or verse, and though often fine is hopelessly drugged on sentimental romance. That is of no consequence: the best writers are flawed. A writer who has one reader seventy years later can rightly be called an artist, and the *Midnight Folk* was published the year I was born. I am the only person left alive to whom Bitterne Manor House, filled with witches, is a place of love. That is why this parenthesis has been written. As will be seen, this house is now utterly obliterated. But small children are still close to God; are often both clairvoyant and clairaudient. As a rule they lose this quickly, but it is often seen that they keep things, places and people vanished from the earth, intact. A child is the historian of the metaphysical. The artist, in this instance Masefield, out of his own memories of a house where he had known happiness, made a mystical marriage with a child, in this instance myself. There are many such other worlds – we are told that they are infinite, and that Nineveh and Troy have not vanished. Our tragedy as human beings is to become progressively dulled and blunted by the noise, the tedious bustle of the moment. There are, for luck has been with me, mornings here in the garden, before the first car comes down the hill to fill the valley with diesel exhaust. Sometimes I have seen

Mr Masefield standing there staring – scribbling in his little notebook.

*

By 1935 Nancy already had a formidable collection of Roman collars. How, where, did she winkle them all out? Most seem in these years to have been Italian – the Missionary Fathers of Verona are strongly present, I must say mysteriously, since what were they doing in England, since their Mission was to bring backward black peoples into the ways of the Lord? I must believe it was to do with the expansionist notions of Il Duce, since there were even two blackavised and formidably bearded bishops: Negri and Beni, mighty fighters for the Faith in northern Africa.

One must be singled out because, as I now know, he was the greatest love affair of Nancy's life. Amleto, in English called Hamlet, had laboured in – vaguely – the Sudan, among a people called Shilluk. He spoke of them with love and understanding. Perhaps he had been sent to rest – but why to England? He spoke always and with longing of going back.

They would be seen, hastening up the garden path, pausing to lift their hat (invariably soft-spoken and polite), get sort of smuggled up to her sitting-room – where the curtains were often drawn, a dim religious light to go with the tea. Crouch in front of that horrid gas fire, talk interminably. About what? God, yes. What Else? Sex? I think yes, in odd ways, far from madonnas who turn out to be the local greengrocer's girl and certainly the painter's mistress. Turn that upside down; the putative mistresses were really all madonnas. What did they? – since for sure she knew nothing of philosophy nor theology – but they kept coming back for more.

Hamlet was the chief of the tribe, tall and handsome, civilized, funny and at ease with children, wearing clerical blacks as though they were a leopardskin. Him we liked. And here comes an odd rustic interlude, almost as though written by

D. H. Lawrence. We used to borrow a cottage in Sussex for summer holidays, remote, rustic, heavenly (paraffin lamp, Primus stove) always known as 'Burwash' – a mile or so upstream of the Kipling house – and she would read aloud from the *Puck* books, emotionally and embarrassingly espressivo. One year Hamlet too came with us; Walter did not. All I can remember is that he borrowed a shotgun and hunted rabbits. We ate a great many rabbits: as in *The Midnight Folk* –

> And Saturday will be Batter-Day
> And Sunday hot-rabbit-pie-day.'

This pastoral is confused in the child's mind with other years, but the odd thing surely is that he should have come at all.

Sure enough, back in Southampton one day this familiar figure drifted in announcing that he had come to say good-bye; it was back to Africa. He produced some exquisite keepsakes; the child got a pair of lovely little ivory elephants, his sister a splendidly wicked paper-cutter whose handle was a crocodile, and Nancy two bigger trunk-upcurling elephants with candlesticks on their backs which would stand for ever after on many mantelpieces. But there was an appalling scene with storms of tears: the child fled from this and knows no more. The name I think was never again mentioned.

But woe's me, there was soon a successor. One must suspect a bout of genuine insanity along this period. Not, perhaps, an illness clinically so to be diagnosed. Again, other experiences have shown me, as a writer, that anyone is capable of anything, at any time, and that talk of insanity is glibly over-facile. She had the overwhelming need for emotional outpouring that among people of great religious fervour produces violent excesses: miracles, stigmata, and the like. Adultery in any physical sense is unthinkable: she announced indeed that this one was her adopted son.

It must have been the year of Munich. We were all very

strung-up. The Spanish Civil War was raging. All of Nancy's old communist lovers had gone to fight, causing havoc since the poor silly girl had been led by Catholic propaganda into seeing Franco as a strong deliverer. We had hardly got rid of Mrs Simpson. Friends coming back from France, from Germany or Austria – 'Harry', most faithful of lovers, was a pillar of the Salzburg Festival – had the most ominous tales.

Certain in my mind is that this new young man put the lid on things for Walter and finally drove him from the house. This was not earlier than 1938, since a magnificent memory is of Walter taking the child (on an Isle of Wight ferry, glorious paddle-wheel Dickensian teuf-teuf) touring round the Coronation Review at Spithead of the warships of every nation gathered to do honour to the King Emperor. No one would ever again see the like of this sight. And Walter, I am happy to say laughing full throat and heart at the famous BBC gaffe, the reporter who got drunk and kept saying 'The Fleet's all lit-up...' The battle-cruisers of every nation and the whole magnificent boiling to be sunk within a year or two. It is alas the last of my few glimpses of Walter whom I loved and did not know. But my son Hugo has grown a short naval beard and looks at forty very like the father this child would come so sorely to miss.

The new young man, a pale thin Irish boy, was glamorous – a Père Blanc, the noble invention of Cardinal Lavigerie to turn the wild Touareg into the ways of God, more lastingly than could spahi or légionnaire or Marshal Lyautey. They wear the white burnous to show that they belong to the Garden of Allah. A handful of dates, a palmful of water. Until a very few years ago they were respected by the most fanatic of Islam throat-slitters.

He had, we were told, to have a 'serious' operation' (antrums, septum, sinus cavities, in those days an unqualified butchery). Following this horror, he would be installed in our guest bedroom and Nancy would do the nursing. So that I remember her, the slim vivid figure, fit for a white burnous, tirelessly running up and down the ladder. Inevitably, the physical reaction was of the utmost brutality. With the beloved's convalescence (pale, needing a shave, in a Bath chair) Nancy collapsed with a heart attack.

The head of the family was called; her elder brother, Eardley, 'The Doctor'. And with pomp, as always, Eardley pronounced that our astoundingly active mother would be from now on forever laid low, a permanent invalid, the heart most gravely strained, to be looked after and cosseted.

The result will be seen. Meantime, most bitter was the child's hatred for the inoffensive young man who had brought our glorious Nancy to this miserable pass. Send that little bugger back to Tunis or wherever it is he comes from.

But first, an anecdote. Because whatever she did and however awful, she never lost the sense of funniness, and her huge peal of laughter would ring out ... In the mid-1930s she had not yet learned to laugh at the Duce. She is in Italy which she loves, in hot pursuit of Saint Francis, a figure who greatly appeals. Most probably she is in Assisi; the great church with the Giotto frescoes and there is also a massive monastery. I should rather have thought that women were not allowed in the guest-house, but she could talk her way in anywhere. Nancy had probably eaten too much pasta, found herself caught short. The Father-Guestmaster, a cheerful soul, led her by devious ways, Franciscan sanitation being summary, but the lavatory when reached was in occupation. Nancy dancing, the holy man soothing. Being Italian he applied his ear to the door, and with a winning smile – 'Won't be long, Signora. I can Hear the Paper'. This became a notable party-piece.

Most horrible was to see the slim burning woman suddenly become slow and heavy. It was 1939.

4

NANCY'S LAST AND PERHAPS WORST ESCAPADE

THIS STORY NEEDS SOME PREPARATION and a look into history. Like everything Nancy did it was comic, but there is tragedy too, because her children were carried away with her. I have – to this day – difficulty in digesting it, though I think I can now understand.

The scene is already set. Her young man, restored to health, has pushed off back to North Africa. Walter has disappeared and I do not know where he is – did she? Her elder daughter, brilliant young woman, has done a Ph.D. on – to be sure – the Arthurian legend, is a specialist in old-French, and is launched upon an academic career. Her younger daughter is a student, midway through the Arts Faculty at the University of Southampton. Her son, who is now eleven, is at a Jesuit preparatory school and thought well of as scholarship material. An examination this summer will doubtless open the doors of Ampleforth or Downside. Walter would not have suggested Holt, I think, but had hopes of Eton as a King's Scholar: I have thought and often of where this might have led. She had, of course, set her face against this. They aren't Catholic. But meantime the child at least is happy and absorbing knowledge. We were all being issued with gas masks, and high in the air above Hampshire the first Spitfire planes could sometimes be seen. The international news appeared ominous. Nancy, in a deck-chair on the grass in this fine weather, is meditating. She has become interested in the tale, overwhelmingly romantic and calculated to appeal to her, of her cousin Erskine Childers.

This is still not widely known to the English, so that I will try to recap the salient features. Erskine (the name was given to the second son, as Eardley to the eldest), after the conventional upbringing suitable to young men of good family, had volunteered for the South African war, written a book about this, Hentyishly called *In the Ranks of the C.I.V.*, which had attracted some notice, and acquired a passable post as a clerk to the House of Commons. All perfectly respectable. His great passion was sailing small boats, and with his wife as crew he had explored the then little-known estuaries and sandbanks of the German North Sea coastline. Out of this came (he had certainly literary talent) that astonishing and splendid spy story, the *Riddle of the Sands*. There was a lot of truth in this. The Kaiser did indeed cherish a notion that in the event of war an invasion of England along the lines described might be envisaged. Erskine commanded sufficient respect for his adventure to be taken seriously, and the result was the formation of the Royal Navy's Volunteer Reserve, in which he was a moving spirit. It is plain that he was imbued with the strongest sense of patriotism as well as gallantry. How this came subtly to be turned in a new direction is something of an enigma. It is generally held that he was influenced by his wife, an Irish-American woman of fanatic tendency. I think it must be remembered that he was very like his cousin Nancy. Great ones for a romantic cause. But whatever the mechanisms, the result was spectacular.

Irish nationalism in the years leading up to 1914 was renascent and strengthening with the defeat of Gladstone's plans to grant Home Rule. It was felt that England would never let go of Ireland, and that violent revolution was the only possible means of wresting this unhappy country from overlordship. A smallish group, but of intense fervour, was planning the insurrection which would become the Easter Rising of 1916. One of their troubles was the lack of arms. This need was made the more urgent by the work of a richer, better organized and more influential group in Ulster, led by Sir Edward Carson, a formidable figure who had determined that Ulster at least would not abandon fidelity to the Crown, and to this end had brought off an extremely good stroke, smuggling a cargo of rifles in to the port of Larne and distributing these arms to the faithful.

Erskine determined that he would do as much on the other side. The *Dulcibella* was a small boat and could not carry much, but a cargo of rifles was assembled. Erskine's sailing skills evaded naval patrols, and his pathetic freight was landed, at Howth just north of Dublin. One of the enthusiasts who helped unload was a thin, burning schoolmaster named Éamon de Valera.

This had far-reaching results. The symbolic but formidable gesture (at the least, the Dublin Brigade of the IRA now had some arms) threw Erskine into whole-hearted acceptance of the fight.

Treason? In a narrow legalistic sense, certainly: Carson, an advocate of fame, would so forcibly have argued. To supply arms is the same as to bear arms against one's country, which Erskine never did. We do not hear of him during the Easter Rising. I think that his own argument would have been that natural justice has more weight than legal definition and that his sense of honour was not compromised: he had acted openly, doing what he thought right. One would compare the trial of Casement, who was hanged, but that was in wartime.

He declared himself an Irishman from then on. One remembers also that many Irishmen of republican convictions saw nothing inconsistent about serving in the Army, wearing British uniform, and this in both wars. It is also interesting that the leaders of the 1916 Rising were executed, save only de Valera, on the technicality of his American citizenship. And it is tragic that many of the Irish leaders refused to accept Erskine. Arthur Griffith to his dying day would never trust 'the damned Englishman'.

He reappears during the Treaty negotiations, where he was secretary to the Irish delegation headed by Griffith and Collins. This post I think was offered on account of his

House of Commons experience. His personal knowledge of the English delegates, Lloyd George, Churchill, Birkenhead, would be valuable and perhaps influential. It is interesting that he argued stubbornly and consistently against accepting the English offers, and when the Treaty was signed he refused to agree to the terms. He was, I suspect, thought of as 'De Valera's man'. Notoriously, despite his political talents and the enormous prestige of being the only surviving chief of the Rising, De Valera was not a delegate, claiming vague obligations to do with fund-raising in America.

It is history that the Treaty was long and bitterly debated in the Irish Parliament, the Dáil, and that when the final vote was narrowly in favour of accepting the Free State, de Valera and many more declared that they would never agree and would continue to fight for the Republic against their former comrades; the result was the Civil War.

In the early stages, much of the civil war was a joke. Men of chivalry, generous men with a strong sense of their own and others' honour, disliked the shedding of blood; a great many bullets were fired in the air. People surrendered, were taken prisoner and promptly let go again. Some, wavering in their convictions, even changed sides. Even after the fierce fighting in Dublin, when the legitimate government troops advanced to reduce the Republican redoubt in the south, generosity often prevailed. Those who had shoulder-to-shoulder fought English troops, the Auxiliaries and the Black and Tans, hated to find themselves killing friends they knew and loved and had suffered with. Dan Breen turning his gun against Michael Collins? But slowly, a merciless bitterness came to obtain.

History: Collins was ambushed on a dirty little road in his own West Cork. Some said killed by accident, others said assassinated. General Richard Mulcahy took his place as commander. Even then there was a jaunty, very Irish slogan. 'Move over, Mick. Make room for Dick.' It is said indeed – an anecdote – that the men Collins had interned in the grim old Maryborough prison went on their knees when they heard the news – to pray for the soul of the Big Fellow. Mulcahy was a thorough-paced professional and pursued the Republicans with vigour. The end makes sad reading. There was some very dirty work in Kerry. So much and so dirty that the Minister of Justice, Kevin O'Higgins, a notable tough, in the long run made a decree, of great severity and – who knows? – justified: that any known Republican sympathizer caught bearing arms would be shot henceforth with no further process of law. This is relevant to Erskine Childers.

He had been named Director of Propaganda in the Republican cause. We may certainly assume that of all people he would refuse to bear arms against a man he loved and respected – Collins. Griffith, heartbroken, had died. Erskine scurried about, generally in hiding and always clandestine like any other guerilla, with his printing press – his job was to produce papers stating and arguing the cause. It makes a pathetic picture. Just recall: his chief, the famous freedom-fighter, Éamon de Valera, spent the entire civil war skulking in hiding declaring himself a mere private soldier. Leadership in the field was left to the generous idealists like Liam Lynch. I find it very difficult to understand how loyalty and devotion is to be given to this lifelong expert in chicanery. Collins, the 'chief terrorist' who had held Dublin throughout the Tan War against the whole apparatus of English rule which added spies and assassins to the brutal police repression, sat down at the table of negotiation with the English delegates. It is on record: Lloyd George, Churchill, Birkenhead, gave way first to the charm, courage, humour of the horrible terror-fighter. They learned to admire, then to respect, finally to accept in friendship and honour this remarkable man. When Collins died in those villainous West Cork hills, Birkenhead, the foremost English jurist, the famous F. E. Smith, was quick to make public utterance – to say 'I have lost a loved friend'. I do not know Erskine's sentiments but I have no doubt that only the awkward, harsh and painful sense of honour divided the two men.

A pathetic end. Childers was arrested by the Free State soldiers. He had in his possession (one can hardly call it 'carrying') a ridiculous little Mickey Mouse pistol, given him – no doubt in joke – by Collins ... Technically thus coming within the prohibition I spoke of. I should like to think that Kevin O'Higgins signed the execution order of an honourable idealist against his wish. There were those who hated Childers. Some of them would have refused to bend their own conscience and their own sense of personal honour.

So they put Erskine in front of the firing squad. There is a romantic anecdote that they put dawn an hour forward so that he could see the sun rise on a free Ireland: also that he shook hands with the soldiers. If true then very Irish. I think it a pretty good end, and nowise out of keeping with the character. I have seen a photograph of a face plainly narrow and obstinate as well as intensely upright. Such was the man and the legend which were so to catch Nancy's breath. Nobody ever shot de Valera, who died full of years and honours amid floods of tears. Another narrow idealist but devious and full of twists, often enough contemptibly so.

Erskine had a son, to be rewarded by de Valera with minor posts as minister in governments. Many years later Ireland, shuffling and coughing rather, elected him President, an honorary position he was given little time to invigorate, since shortly afterwards a heart attack put an end to him. It was to this country, with a welcome from this cousin, that Nancy bolted in 1939 carrying two children with her.

It is now sixty years since this happened. During that time I have ranged from burning fury, hatred of this utter irresponsibility and contempt for this cowardly and selfish flight, to sympathy and understanding and – if this be not vanity – forgiveness.

Typically she found a cottage in the countryside (taken of course unseen). Typically, this had to be in the most romantic of places among the Ryans of Tipperary, a mighty clan and of every imaginable complexion. The local deputy to the

Dáil, man after her own heart, straight out of a Western, was Dan Breen, famous freedom-fighter, by then laid low through many wars and fearful wounds but far from the 'shadow of a gunman'. One could be reminded of Nancy herself. Of him legend would recount that heated words passed in the Dáil; that Breen, insulted, would invite his opponent to step out-side. 'For God has seen fit to put me in a wheelchair, but a man called Colt invented a way of seeing everyone on an equal footing.' Breen was not the sort of man to have ordered Erskine Childers shot. Plenty of the men of 1921 were still alive, and so were their emotions. Thus, I can very well re-member de Valera, then Premier, tearing in from Blackrock in a convoy of three big black sedans all full of pistol-packing bodyguards. There were men of high quality such as Mulcahy or MacEoin ready to serve their country under law, but there were those too who had neither forgotten nor for-given the death of Collins: and even today there are voices to call it assassination, and one plotted by de Valera. The child in 1939 knew nothing of this; understood nothing of these new surroundings – much as though he had suddenly been dumped in Bogotá . . .

To a child like this the Irish Mail was as romantic a train as the Orient Express. Euston – the old and famous Euston of the Arch and a colossal stink of dust and fish; mourned by Betjeman. London, Midland, & Scottish, stops at Rugby, Crewe and Chester, for the Holyhead–Kingstown ferry. Kingstown, one had now to say Dun Laoghaire, pronounced Dunleary, was the gateway to Dublin Bay, most beautiful in a chill August dawn. A charming clunking little train brought one into the heart of Dublin within twenty minutes. Impossible to believe that this time yesterday he was getting up and dressing in Bitterne Manor House.

Like the opening page of *Treasure Island* – I remember it as though it were yesterday. The grim little station of Westland Row. A line of cabs drawn by poor old nags; four-wheelers, musty straw and mouldy leather, red-nosed Jarvey

in a black coat gone green. Perfectly Victorian and so was the
Hotel Pelletier in Harcourt St. Breakfast in a smell of old
ladies, with them all about one reading the paper. 'No war
yet today, dear' – it would be another three days. It was I
think the Terenure tram that brought one to the General
Post Office in O'Connell Street, a vast pompous pile where
the child crossed a sombre stony hall to poste restante, passing a fearful emotional monument to the Heroes of 1916,
who had (most ill-advisedly) chosen this symbolic pile to oc-
cupy, in revolt against Us. But the Us was now They. And
we have left They behind, arming to fight Nazi Germany.
Today I – who is I? – am suddenly no longer concerned.
Gone through the looking-glass. Disoriented is not a child's
word. Nancy, belting about, looking for a kirby-grip to keep
her hair tidy, is a sort of Red Queen.

It was Victorianly, Dickensianly poor. Thin, pale, barefoot
children everywhere, and the shawlies. The Pillar, where the
trams turned round – good god, Admiral Nelson, what is he
doing here? (He went on standing there, higher and more
massive than in Trafalgar Square, gazing down Sackville
Street, resisting all attempts to blow him up, until 1960.)
The huge Georgian buildings are still there, classical pillared
architraved majesty, bullet scarred; the Customs House and
the Four Courts of great formal beauty.

One did not go north of the rotunda, because of the
slums: dread. The splendid Georgian houses of Mountjoy
Square were derelict, with all the windows broken and slum
children sitting on the steps showing very grubby knickers.
The Seán O'Casey characters lived here but one was allowed
to meet them only on the stage of the Abbey Theatre. It
would be four years before I would walk at night all over
Dublin, and even then I did not know that Leopold Bloom
had lived in Dorset Street because James Joyce was greatly
frowned upon: de Valera's Ireland was incredibly prudish
and small-minded. We knew only the South Side, and only
the very narrow strip of that from Stephens Green through

47

the snobbish (doctors, lawyers) squares, down Baggot Street and Leeson Street into the respectable districts of Ballsbridge and Donnybrook, as far as Ailesbury Road.

As for our cousin Erskine, he lived out in Rathgar, 'nice, refined Rathgar'. When glimpsed he was polite. I suspect, now, he had been horrified by this appalling woman, hideously raffish, shatteringly outspoken, over-enthusiastic, not-to-be-frequented woman. He might still have been trying to live down his own parents, who had caused enough trouble . . . But Nancy is in a hurry, to go and live 'down the country', among the real Irish. The Ballsbridge world, centred round the fine buildings and grounds of the Royal Dublin Society, was too Anglo, too Protestant and far too respectable for her tastes. It would be another two years before she would come back here.

The effect upon the child may be guessed; calamitous. Something will have to be said about the appalling school, the utter desolation, for this is also part of 'The Tale of Anne D.'. But for now – 'When is my father coming?' – he had no suspicion that Walter's increasingly long absences had hardened into separation. 'No doubt a little later.' Cowardice disguised as tact. It was a month and more later before she found the courage to tell that Walter was dead. In some London hospital; I have never known where. The heart had given out at last; one cannot feel surprise. But the shattered child was alone in a green land of savages. England was at war, and the boy sent to boarding-school while Nancy indulged herself in ripe sentimentalities among the Ryans of Tipperary.

Back in Southampton it was the eldest sister's task to sort out and send on the furniture, the books (she made some very odd choices and much would be mourned), the bibelots reflecting various religious enthusiasms: the rest and the best went to the sale-room. One must pause, a second, to say that in 1940 Southampton, important centre of shipping and production, was heavily attacked by the Luftwaffe. A stray heavy landed plonk in the centre of Bitterne Manor House (lying in that vulnerable, targeted loop of the river). Thereafter there was nothing but a heap of rubble. It would be left to the English to demolish those great gaunt walls, to sweep it all away years later, to clear the terrain which had seen the magic, to allow speculators to build a very exclusive development for wealthy folk. Yes, I once went back, damned fool. 'Ichabod O'Man' as Mr Polly had rather often occasion to say.

The younger sister, now in her twenties, patient and sweet-natured girl, seems not to have complained. Of the university there would be no more question; her task was simple, to keep house for the still occasionally roaring Mama, who would live here the last fragments of the old gusto. Rather portly, much reduced but still exuberant, bravely walking if needing a push uphill, Nancy was greatly enjoying the green Tipperary countryside. The house, a pleasant simple foursquare Georgian cottage, was the house of the bailiff or overseer for a quite large and still intact Anglo-Irish estate. Many of these manors were attacked and burned during The Troubles but many had survived, generally through luck. Many of these houses were historic; some were beautiful. There were owners who had been just and kindly towards their tenantry. The village was only a street of primitive shielings. In one lived Mick, the ploughman, and his father, old Patrick, in that next door. There were many children. The only room was swept and scrubbed. The fire heated the pot. The pot held potatoes. The potatoes when cooked were put on the table peeled and eaten. I do not know of any change that had taken place in this way of life inside a century. The children were neat, alert and well-mannered. I could see no difference from such country people as we had known in France or in England.

Nancy spent much time in Mick's kitchen. She became greatly attached to Mrs Mick, a quiet thin woman of striking dignity and beautiful manners. Mick was tall, handsome, talkative and funny. Old Patrick was of different character, still and reserved but with an antique turn of speech, most strikingly vivid, rich and racy. With these people she was on the happiest terms. No social barrier whatever obtained between them and the assured but never arrogant Englishwoman of the loud commanding upper-class voice. There was a mutual respect. In neither was there any shadow of pretension or meanness of spirit. In neither was there vulgarity. No doubt she was ridiculous. Miss Bates is ridiculous; she is also a simple, good and generous woman. Mr Woodhouse is ridiculous and a gentle, kind, polite old man. Mrs Elton is an ill-bred, pushing, vulgar woman. She would not have lasted long in an Irish village.

Nancy's house was perfectly adequate in size, proportion and Victorian conveniences. There were three good, sunny living-rooms and a stone-flagged kitchen. Upstairs were four bedrooms (one for the maid, a nice girl called Kitty) and a bathroom. There was a small neat garden with grass and flower-beds. My sister found housekeeping strenuous but manageable. For shopping she bicycled to the little country town, four miles off. There were many difficulties, and much in wartime not to be found, but no real hardship. Social life consisted of the village and this was no hardship either.

There is one detail I think worth remembering. Nancy's mother was old and felt herself isolated; it was arranged that she should come to live with her daughter. De Valera had refused to honour the agreement to allow England the use of Irish naval bases, the 'Treaty Ports', but in all other respects the terms were kept to, however grudgingly. Certainly the communications between the two countries never broke down. Clare Childers passed the last year of her life here, I think in happiness with her daughter and granddaughter she loved. The old lady died in peace and Nancy had a stone inscribed with a noble old text. 'Her children rose up and called her blessèd.' In the little cemetery of Templemore, this might still be there: Ireland would not dishonour the name.

Nancy cleared the smooth stone floor of the kitchen and gave a dance. This was a social event of importance and the whole village came, even the blacksmith's daughters: he was a craftsman and a Protestant, both separate from and above the peasantry, but Dorrie and Sadie were the two prettiest girls for miles around. The best accordion-player of the district, the best fiddler, were engaged for the music. Protocol was strict as for a wake: tea and cake for the women, bottles of stout for the men, whiskey only for the older patriarchs like Patrick.

The rules for country dancing were equally strict. One will be reminded again of disgusting Mr Elton refusing to dance with Harriet, and Mr Knightley instantly leading her out. The boy, thirteen, had just enough social sense to ask Mrs Mick to stand up (the perfect partner, of outstanding tact and delicacy, feather light guiding the clumsy child). Upon which Mick, elegant in manner as Frank Churchill, advanced upon my sister. His boots turn as fast, clack as sharp as an Andalusian gypsy; he whirls at such speed that she gasps to me in French – '*Est-ce que ma culotte se voit?*' He is the star of the occasion and between dances he sings; he has some six songs and a robust pub tenor for 'The Yellow Rose of Texas' and to be sure 'Mick MacGilligan's daughter Mary-Anne'. Nancy who is enjoying herself enormously calls out 'Splendid, you must have some whiskey' and a very soft gentle voice says 'No, Mick'. His wife can show herself more of a lady than her hostess.

It is sad that this pastoral would be brief. She began to feel unexplained pains in the gut, and the local doctor, while mumbling vaguely about colitis (fashionable jargon-word of the time), had sense enough to insist that she consult a Dublin specialist. Professor Henry Moore was the man in internal medicine. This was something to be done in style, with panache. She took a small, pleasant flat in Georgian Waterloo Road and assembled a new court among the faculty, all subjugated by her charm and blaze. I think she had missed the stimulus of intellectual company. There were of course several distinguished Roman collars, silky in manner as in theology, and Erskine reappeared, introducing a number of shining lights in law of social affairs. Doctors were by long tradition the centre of Dublin society; one thinks of Wilde and Gogarty. The top of the profession was sophisticated and witty, and flocked to her door. I am happy to think that this short year was a whirl of gaiety and for her unending amusement. At last she was in her true element. Naturally, for her trouble only the most eminent would do, and 'dear Henry' brought the wonderful courtly neurologist Abrahams and Andrew Butler, the 'best surgeon in Dublin'. For she had a bad, and worsening, intestinal cancer but pain was dismissed with gallantry as well as showmanship. I think this year shows her at her best: for the role of queen she was perfectly cast.

In retrospect, 'dear Henry' seems to have taken a very long time in making his diagnosis, and to have been extremely leisurely in preparing her for his own special private nursing home next door to the Mater Hospital. I rather suspect that he thought her condemned, and wished to prolong the gaiety for as long as pain would allow. But a Nancy stupefied by morphia would have no fun, and there came the day when 'dear Andy' would wheel her in to a theatre where laughs were infrequent. 'Remember, Andrew, if I do wake up, I want you to be there, with champagne. And oysters' – a vague idea of what would be fitting. She did: he was. I remember him; big fine ugly man with orange bristles on the forearms and a noble delicacy in the massive pianist's hands. He took most of her lower belly and she lived twenty more years astounding every doctor who came near.

It is difficult not to sentimentalize the final years, of Nancy on her back – between the dodgy heart and the missing bowels there was often no fun at all, and we had to learn to give her hypodermics in bouts of darkened-room through many bitter days. But often too sitting up, standing up, dressing

(the shapeless clothes were now more than royal caprice) –
even sallying out to restaurants, theatre or the cinema. The
boy, growing up, squired her to these small pleasures, and so
did many friends, some from Bloomsbury days. She liked
expensive places, where she could be sure of being treated as
though she were a princess. This in Dublin meant the
Shelbourne Hotel or the Royal Hibernian. It can't be called
vanity or snobbery: innocent enjoyment of a pack of headwaiters, there to pick up a dropped table napkin or look up a
phone number.

She liked to be ferried over to London to stay with her
brother The Doctor, immensely rich through the very best
kind of Primrose Hill practise. Eardley, notoriously parsimonious (given to supping off a cold sausage) did not take her
to Claridges or Boulestin; the pleasures in this house were
Fabianly intellectual ('We're all going to be very quiet and
listen to the Brains Trust') and it was never explained how
these pure principles were reconciled with a famous and lu-
crative bedside manner. His friends were austere, of political
and philosophic persuasion, Malcolm Muggeridge or Frank
Pakenham, and much that was happily reminiscent of communist salad days: it would have been greatly to her taste to
send them to Confession and a certainty of the Resurrection.

But being Nancy she gathered innumerable lame ducks,
pederast book reviewers and tormented poets, heroin users
and Indian mystics who had taken the wrong path to enlight-
enment: Eardley soothing the soma while Nancy wrestled
with the psyche. I suppose I sound sarcastic but I do not
exaggerate. I would be astonished in future years but much
edified to be told by some distraught television star with a
lifelong habit of touching up choirboys how much she had
helped and how gratefully he had loved her. I did not understand. I am not at all sure I do now. This wayward silly
woman was good, gentle, wise. I never believed it. Men and
women famous then, or once, or later to become so, have
told me what they owed her. I could wish that she might

have spared some of this wisdom for her son, as silly as herself. I am so very like her. She found it, I suppose, impossible to speak with me. I found her shaming because I was ashamed of myself.

Did she know, herself, that she was a healer, a Sophia? Any more than she had ever realized what a foolish, extravagant and destructive woman she had been? I cannot answer and I shall not try. She knew certainly that the restless genes were damaging, and most to those who carried them. She suffered much in body and in soul. Though I know now much more than I did I must obey reticence; I must respect dignity, decency, privacy. The writer has the vile itch to know what lies behind the image, and is here inhibited since it is also so much a mirror image. There are things here that I must not toy with nor diminish. I have not myself, perhaps, as yet suffered enough to see this woman – she was my mother – clearly.

She made amends. Her daughter, snatched from studenthood at twenty-one years of age and abused for another twenty as domestic slavey ('Dear, I seem to have lost my glasses' or just 'Pass me my red shawl', had trained herself in modern methods of educating small children – in the 1940s, Madame Montessori was seen as a startling pioneer and all that is now nursery commonplace was then beyond the comprehension of the holy nuns entrusted with schooling tasks. The young woman wanted to have a school of her own. It is to Nancy's credit to have said, 'Very well dear: I'll buy you a suitable house but this will take the very last scraps of my capital'. One must not call it a poisoned present. The girl, become a remarkable woman, made of this house not a school but a home, taking ten abandoned children from the public orphanages and bringing them up as her own; an astonishing feat made possible by Nancy's loyalty. How her son would fare is another story.

But I have one or two touching memories of the last twilight years in which pain and fatigue did not always conquer.

When I brought my future wife to visit the old woman in the darkened room she perked up visibly, enchanted by this young, blonde, pretty – Dutch – girl equally visibly intimidated by this terrifying antique monument. 'Can you sing?' Indeed the girl could sing, liked nothing better, had carolled past many bitter experiences; too many indeed for a young girl but the ravages of wartime take many forms. 'Sing to me,' said Nancy in the old commanding manner, and the girl did. No Schubert – the simple country Dutch and German songs of her own childhood. 'That was lovely,' said Nancy. 'Children, leave me now, I'm tired.' But she would love her new daughter forever.

I was far away. That had no importance; planes existed to be taken in a hurry. But the telephone voice – 'She's gone' – was for something near, much too near. Sorrow; pain; these are the natural reactions. They had been long expected, and now they were conventional, empty, mechanical. It was the end of the concert; the last chord of the resolution; the close. If there were not to be this final bringing together of the orchestra where would be the point of the symphony? One cannot be left hanging in the air.

I will have to go to my own funeral. That, yes. Time, time, must have a stop. Tomorrow, yes, in the empty concert hall, the cleaning women will plug in the vacuum cleaner, the *Staubzauger*, the gatherer-up of dust. They pass along the rows of stalls, unsurprised at the quantity of debris; old programmes, gloves, handkerchiefs – and now and then something comic which will make them laugh. The music, what has happened to the music? It has not stopped; there is to be sure a pause, shown by a sign in the notation, a well-known sign which has sometimes been engraved on the tombstones of musicians. So that here is written the sign saying 'Pause'.

The meaning of this, as is evident, can only be limited to a crude device. End of story-book. That was 'The Tale of Anne D'.

For how much there is and will be cannot be written. Some facts are known now to science, about genes; their structure understood – so that police laboratories can match samples of blood, sweat, semen or saliva. We can dig up bones and scrape at them, to prove some obscure question of parentage. As long as there remains a fragment of tissue there will be physical facts to be made known. The biochemists can say nothing about metaphysics, which they prefer to pretend does not exist. What can be said about the Childers genes? That my romantic, quixotic cousin Erskine is buried in Irish soil together with his honour, and his son after him – and that this bloodline continues, perhaps – this is much to Hecuba but not to me. That this is part of Irish history, and in turn of the history of Europe and of mankind; that in their turn Clare and Nancy were buried in Ireland – messages for a poet. The bones of the saints have often written poetry.

The Freeling genes, so strong in Nancy and of which, inheriting them, I am continually made aware; these, forcibly are of interest since they shipwrecked her, bid fair to shipwreck her son. A leaky ship ill-steered and carrying too much sail. The forever-restless vagabondage, the wayward irresponsibility, the total incapacity to understand the most elementary grammar of purse and pocket: these are much to me. If I have sought to anchor myself in this house, in this village, I have had good reasons. I have for long wanted to write this book.

Nancy could have been a writer; it was strong in her. It was strong in both her brothers so that one wonders where it came from, how it came about, a strange and wayward wind. Art could even move Eardley, that careful man. By pure coincidence (there was talk of using work of mine as material for a television series) I was in the London house of the putative producer. She had on her walls pictures painted by Eardley, of which I was dismissive – 'goodish amateur Sunday stuff'. Her disagreement may have had a stronger base than my prejudice. I would be forced to say now that there was 'something there of truth' to 'something better than mere tolerably accomplished craftsmanship'. I have read also the memoir he wrote. Professionally I am here on surer ground; it was the typical amateur work of the man who finds himself interesting and feels convinced that a public, a publisher, must agree: they don't. Every publishing office gets these weighty scripts by every post. The fact remains that the Doctor was a better painter than I could give him credit for.

Nancy's younger brother Mike I came to know, to my sorrow, only towards the end of a classically-Freeling career of misfitted uncomprehending prejudice, fear and the child of fear which is hatred. Over a moment lasting at best two years. When he was old, tired, penniless, and still not defeated. For Mike I have no breath of harsh judgment, bitter dealing. He was the 'bad hat' never known in childhood, never seen, spoken of – if at all with bated breath: what on earth does this idiotic cliché mean?

Mike was a homosexual, a pederast, a boy-lover; a collector of Sicilian shepherd-adolescents. Nancy, child of her Edwardian upbringing, never could quite bring herself to swallow this. He wrote a good book about his life, with no breath in it of dishonesty or self-pity; professionally written for he was an excellent journalist, a foreign correspondent for most of his career. This book, in 1965 the first to treat the subject with detachment and humour as well as sensitivity, made an enormous difference to the thousands in England forever ashamed and secretive. Together with Lord Montagu, who had gone to prison with the panache due his name, this straightened many spines. If since then they show rather too much vulgar ostentation, it cannot be laid at the door of these men, who shared a gallant indifference to ignorance and spiteful hypocrisy. Mike of course was Freeling enough to enjoy other countries, and to have a taste for rough country wine I recognized and shared.

Incurably, impenitently a hand-to-mouth man, I suspect

Mike never had a home of his own, his longish life through. Granted, the world of a foreign correspondent is by definition a rackety succession of hotel rooms, borrowed flats, pads and perches the world across. But the human being needs a lair. Even Sir Jocelyn Hitchcock had a bolt-hole somewhere. They have untidy, neglected and uncomfortable places in odd corners of London, Paris or New York – quite possibly all three. They have like everyone else books and pictures, little value-less treasures, objects acquired, and given them, too, by people who have loved them. Oddities from Outer-Mongolia – 'yes I know, it's hideous but I'm attached to it. I might have been a bit pissed at the time'. Quite often these hidey-holes, scarcely meriting the name 'apartment' got bombed or demolished during slum clearance; mysteriously burned down – repossessed by the landlord because the rent hadn't been paid. Everything has disappeared, filched, looted or thrown out as junk. Oh well, there was nothing much any-how, not worth keeping y'know. And one goes on acquiring more. Good thing really to have a purge from time to time.

Often enough, also, some passion for permanence took hold. A moment when one was flush with cash, for they are always either rich or broke. A sudden enthusiasm for the pastoral cottage in Dorset. At one time or another there was probably a wife, who made the place homely, bought furni-ture, haunted antique shops. The drains are suspect; there's always an odd smell. 'I've lost the key but we'll get in some-how.' Between the wars there were many such, picked up for a couple of hundred pounds: the roof sagged, there were damp stains on the ceilings, the 'geyser' never did work prop-erly. Insect life is varied and widespread. You can see where we once did a bit of gardening. Janey, worth a packet today.[3]

To my knowledge, Mike never did. To be sure – even in Dorset, the police might at any moment appear; the homo-sexuals of those days lived always under threat. Some were

---

3. In Ireland but also England 'Janey' was a commonplace euphemism for 'Jesus'. An exact parallel is the well brought-up girl who still says 'Gosh' or 'Golly'.

rich and careful with it, like Willy Maugham, the highly lush existence on Cap d'Antibes – and plenty more, somewhat more primitive but still comfy, in places like Tangier. They all fled Berlin when Hitler arrived, turned up safe and sound in Santa Monica. Mike spread his tent a good deal in North Africa, used often to talk about 'my island' (I think one of the Stromboli group) but could never manage to put down roots: I must conclude that the horrible genes forbade it.

*

Nancy: I could not write this book without her portrait, so essential if I were ever to understand anything at all. The never-ending changes of house, it is apparent, are psychologically the starting point for any effort to come to grips with her son's childhood and adolescence.

She always tried to make a home, however elusive this might prove. I have made it clear that Bitterne Manor House, arguably the dottiest of all homes, was for four magnificent years peace and great happiness. However loony, however infested by witches, a splendid, immensely secure – guarded – house; a home.

When, thus, and this will stand for all the others, she entered the overseer's house in Tipperary (as pastoral as possible) she obeyed the law of the lares and penates. Her elder daughter had saved all that this girl, as eccentric as her mother, thought indispensable. With little fuss or delay, Pickfords brought all this rubbish safely to port. In any English house the central room has a fireplace, and thereby a chimney-piece with perhaps a marble mantel and quite elaborate surrounds. Wherever she found herself, Nancy followed her (by now) immoveable pattern. In the exact centre went a Victorian looking-glass, round in a square, over-elaborate gilded stucco frame (rather chipped by this time). On either side, symmetrically, went the two little silver-points of Freeling forebears and outside those the pretty oval portraits (now restored by my eldest son and hung in my daughter's house) of two Victorian Freeling children. These were sacred. In the centre of the mantelpiece stood her mother's little carriage clock and on either side the two elephant-and-castle candlesticks (ivory they were; African in style they certainly were not) and outside these again two of the dreadful little busts, as displayed in many a suburban drawing-room to show cultural interests; representing Shakespeare and Dickens. Except for the little clock (still made to the original eighteenth-century model) it all looked like a junk-shop in Tottenham Court Road taste. Nancy had no feeling for objects and in her bedroom stood many statues of saints, in the style of sentimental religiosity known as Place St Sulpice (one expected the paperweight which winds up and plays the Lourdes hymn...)

Her clothes from first to last were hewn out of strong thick materials, quite shapeless and seemingly flung at her. Those bought for her children were just as bad, always too large, 'to grow into', ludicrous to look at and shaming to wear. Her housekeeping was erratic, her cooking wonderfully haphazard, since as my sister remarked

> 'Mama's heroes lie in clover
> But hark, the milk is boiling over.'

Vague memories of French meals, dishes taught her by Jeanne or Louise, might lead to complicated ambitions, followed by a sudden lurch towards tinned sardines.

Her manners were lavishly Edwardian; I have seen her entertain a cardinal in the princely style to which no doubt she thought the man accustomed (rather taken aback by the beautiful courtly curtsey and the formal elegance of kissing his ring). 'Tea, Eminenza?' But hers (without milk or sugar) she would be quite likely to pour into the saucer if too hot; totally unselfconscious. She swept in to the kitchen of an Irish cottage as though it were a Venetian palace. Ballroom or stable, the natural, instant centre of attention. Straight of spine, with an odd, regal carriage of the head slightly turned and lifted (and a tiny toss of the head while walking). She could, in company, be witty and extremely funny. I can see her thus, dressed in rags, at a government cocktail party surrounded by senators and ambassadors, all eating out of her hand. I was cringing in a corner, adolescently embarrassed at the fearful carrying English voice (the Irish are soft-spoken) and suddenly filled with pride, so evidently was she not merely the dominant but the most interesting person in the room. Young and slim, she burned, and the face became incandescent. Old, bun-faced and portly, a serene dignity, rather like Victoria at Osborne. At any age, in any surroundings, every man in the room (especially noticeable among the Roman collars) fell instantly in love with her. And nobody was ever less like Sex-Appeal Sarah ('My body gets barer, Each time I appear on the stage'). One can read in Edwardian memoirs about the grand hostesses and tremendous beauties in the magnificent houses, Polesden Lacey or wherever: she must have had a good dash of this since the grand manner never quite left her. Or one can read, from George Bernard Shaw, much of what Ellen Terry brought to a stage or a dressing-room but also to the dingiest sitting-room (or, one is tempted to guess while sitting on the lav). Regnant, or in urban traffic – the bicycle wheel got stuck in the tramline – one had to take her as one found her and, however catastrophic, it was a tidal wave. I jump from piece to piece of the wreckage she made of her youngest child, as one would of a bombed building. I have rancour, hatred and resentment. I laugh acridly at that awful flock of Roman-collared crows, and affectionately at the gang, faithful into old age, often, of the Communist intellectuals; some died in Spain and one at least became a boffin to invent strange weapons against Hitler ... I am saddened, and sobered, to think of Chris, and of the several Walters. 'Poor Chris' was said, in later years, to have written a letter, polite and earnest, to my father, suggesting that Walter marry his mistress: this would somehow make the situation more respectable. I am not sure that this wasn't Nancy's imagination at work.

Hating her, loving her, when at last I got the phone call,

my sister's over-controlled voice saying 'I miss her so' ... leave it at that. 'The Tale of Anne D.' had at last reached a full stop.

*

A home. All too obviously, the boy, now a man and fighting hard to be rid of this monstrous shadow, had never known one. Marrying, it was evident, in the forefront of his mind was the need to find one. There exist, on any roulette wheel, one or two winning numbers, alongside the overwhelming proportion of losers. The good one may be a trap; I refuse the adjective 'treacherous'. One could be tempted to gamble on it. A woman who understands the word 'home' is thereby the more precious, the big prize. All such remarks are inept, to be sure. 'Unsatisfactory' as Captain Queeg's written report was found. 'Tells me nothing I want to know and says nothing I didn't know already.' The amateur psychiatrist, settling gleefully upon the obvious, finds facile explanations for errant behaviour; glib, simplistic and rather childish of him. It is not as easy an equation as all that. The bright child, headstrong, self-willed, impatient, very decided in its instinctive seizing and rejecting, fits into a known pattern; it is visible and audible – physically extremely so. Amused, I can *see* Nancy in her three-year-old great-granddaughter – just such another gifted and obstreperous girl, open, warm and loving. Grandparents, indulgent by definition, like to see these little family resemblances; it flatters their vanity. Quite possibly, some stray gene is there present; environment and upbringing will have a great deal more to say and so will circumstance. Not the least of these, the hundred years of history from then to now. A trivial example, but I believe valid, would be the very different clothes little girls now wear, of a fluidity and simplicity that alters movement and modifies behaviour.

Some things do not change. For a child to lose its father at an early age, in some inexplicable but vaguely disgraceful fashion, must at any moment in history be traumatic. A mother both over-protective and notoriously lacking both tact and judgment is going to add greatly to a child's insecurity; I can testify to that. A broken home is the worst of evils. The abundance of these today inflames and enfevers the misery of so many lives.

Unhesitating, I can trace a long row of failures and inabilities to the upheavals of my own childhood. It is a wise provision in psychoanalysis that the analyst should himself have undergone the professional searching of the psyche. The fiction writer draws freely from his own well of suffering and experience. Torment enriches talent. It has been many times remarked that physical illness tends to diminish our better human qualities. Most of the patients in any hospital become morose and whiny, selfish and greedy. Indeed the writer Somerset Maugham, walking the wards as a medical student, thought that this had given him a permanent bias towards sceptical distrust; that he would never again take better than a jaundiced view of humanity. There is truth in this, if with a reservation or two. I can myself bear witness that Saint Thomas's Hospital was a dreadful place even by Victorian standards: I suffered there as a child from cruelty and brutality. I know also that such places held and hold saints and angels, but any hospital remains the place from which one escapes, fortunate if not feet first. It is not merely the patients who are to blame.

Whereas – equally often noticed – the sufferer from mental illness may be incontinent of violence or urine and may also be fertile in art. It is now at last recognized that arts are therapy – one can be forgiven for remarking that painting or writing takes little in the way of expensive financial outlay.

We accept that 'artists' in the loose general sense are all dotty. Plenty indeed are mad as hatters; few manage to lead what is called a normal life. Their wives, husbands or other relatives who look after them – 'do think of putting on clean socks' – have and need immense resources of patience, that unselfish virtue.

I do not know whether one can call Nancy an artist. Not in any conventional sense; she was not a good writer, knew nothing of painting, was musically illiterate and had little appreciation of the work of others. The turbulent mix of vivid energetic genes, of strong will and much intelligence, of fire and passion and contempt for convention, made of her a remarkable woman.

To gather the facts, as far as I know them, of her life into this brief case history served two purposes. One was to make this woman known to the grandchildren who can scarcely recall her: my daughter, the youngest child, never in fact saw her. The other, equally valid, was to come to a better understanding of myself. That I greatly resembled her was at all times apparent. The child, ridiculously cosseted, the ee-wee lamb kept so closely clutched, received an indelible stamp. Growing up, equally ludicrously neglected, the boy felt it the more after losing his own father. The simultaneous trauma of 1939, snatched away from every stabilizing influence, made further ravages (much of the charm of Ireland is in the inconsequential and alas from colonial times the irresponsible: the alloy of harsh insensitive repression and paternalist amusement has been much commented). The Freeling genes were early noticed and egoistically applauded. Great-Aunt Annie had been excited to see these come out strongly in 'darling Nance': they were greeted with the same enthusiasm in her son. The more perhaps since his two sisters, all right, half-sisters, were plainly of different blood, while poor unlucky Walter could see very little of himself in this boy, who couldn't hold a bat straight, could scarcely swim, and was probably gun-shy (as an Army recruit, to my own amazement I turned out the best shot in the squad, while screamed at by drill-sergeants as impossibly awkward and sleepy).

Lastly, in old age it was noticed that I became, physically, the spitting image of my mother: 'portly' (to be polite); even the toss of the head and swing of the left arm when walking. The loud, commanding Cambridge 1920s voice which has made journalists snigger. The tendency to say 'I can't find my glasses darling'. It is a heavy burden to carry, which I have had to learn to accept, and be grateful for.

But this must not lead me into 'autobiography'. Heavens sakes, nothing is more boring nor more futile, just as nothing else so shows up the pompous self-importance that my uncle Mike so loathed in his elder brother, the Doctor.

I have chosen thus to follow and examine the one thread that binds me unbreakably to the Edwardian beginnings: 'the house'. Which, in turn, is part of 'the village'.

Must I thus not prelude my effort to see the village (in its own context, disinfected of my now forty years' presence) with a page of explanation?

5

PRELUDE TO THE VILLAGE

THE 'I' WAS LIVING IN ENGLAND, the antique and noble town of Bristol, once the second city of the country, still a splendid place. We had a large magnificent flat on the first floor of a fine Georgian house: one climbed the steep hill and came out in Clifton. I had an excellent undemanding job as sous-chef in the town's big hotel. Little work, save to oversee and organize other cooks, take the place of the chef when absent, make things run smoothly. For this my skills and experience were adequate. Indeed – in a sudden emergency – I could defend kitchen honour well enough to be congratulated: a happy manager told me that I had saved his job. This praise was already hollow: I knew myself a good cook, a competent second-in-command, and I knew also that my physical deficiency of energy (easy enough to hide) would never let me reach further in this profession which had been mine for twelve years: in a hotel or restaurant of any worth the physical effort is of more importance than manual skills or craftsmanly imagination and execution. I felt indifference; ninety per cent of my energy was already elsewhere.

The purpose of that trivial anecdote is two-fold. Firstly, that here was a man of thirty-five, with three children and his wife pregnant with a fourth; an age, and a situation, when one is mature and can be expected to behave responsibly and with some prudence. He had a reasonable job, earning an adequate wage and doing little enough for it: he was liked by his subordinates and valued by his chiefs. When, thus, a sudden piece of good fortune, akin to winning the lottery, comes his way, one might expect that he would have the sense to hold on to his position while he looked about him and made a few plans. No Freeling alas ever did anything sensible.

Bolted, and if not in a Nancy sense then with quite as much precipitation and fundamental idiocy.

Secondly, the nature of this good fortune was to be less arbitrary and more gradual than a win on the Lotto. For two years and more he had been writing. The student of Joseph Conrad's life will recall that after some years as an officer in the Merchant Marine and getting at last his Captain's ticket, he was one day sitting in a London boarding-house, between jobs and hoping for a ship, when for no apparent reason he took pen and paper and began with *Almayer's Folly*. He has described further moments – the café in frozen Amsterdam, a wharfside in Rouen – when kept hanging about in difficulties with the cargo or the Customs, he went on writing. The vocation can speak in this insistent voice at any time in a man's life, and under any circumstances.

This young man had no very clear idea how to write a book and the crime theme was purely instinctive. He managed to complete it and sent the manuscript to a London agent. Was surprised to get a courteous answer inviting him to come and talk this over. To meet people over lunch, to be told that the book was good, that it would be a success. Good heavens, he was even paid some money.

The agent, woman of distinction, eminent in her profession, told him that one more or less successful book was neither here nor there. The difficulty was always with the second, for this would be the touchstone in deciding whether he was a real writer. To pay no attention to publishers; go home and write another. Which he did, very happy with the enthusiasm shown in London, in New York, in Paris and a dozen more capitals; now he was on his way.

The comparison with Conrad, fortuitous, seemed to him significant. This was Walter's favourite writer, and leaving behind what must have been seen as a failed life and a hopeless domestic tangle, in 1938, he took one book with him, Conrad's *Chance*: I see it now with sadness as a significant choice. The young Polish enthusiast, after some years in

France and a few wastefully silly adventures, had come to England with the determination to study for – and get – his second mate's ticket through the exacting and difficult examination demanded and to make his way as a ship's officer. He scarcely spoke English; he would find the speaking difficult all his life. When it came to putting words on paper, a bitter and laborious struggle, for many years ill-rewarded, he had to grit his teeth. Nothing and nobody could take away his personal achievement, Master Mariner, with his three certificates, second mate, first mate and Captain under the red ensign; a tremendous win against heavy odds. For varying reasons it was very difficult to get ships. But was he perhaps a writer, rather than (perhaps over and above) a sailor? He had a couple of good friends, who told him that this was so. Most notably Edward Garnett, distinguished (and influential) man of letters, publishers' reader and advisor whose word counted for much. I can take notice hereabouts of a far-reaching difference – quite apart from talent – between his situation and my own. Logically and naturally, in his early writing, Conrad turned to his Far-Eastern experiences, as mate and skipper of trading ships tramping from island to island in the hunt for a profitable cargo. This for publishers was good stuff, juicy, enticingly exotic (it would be long before there were many readers for success came to him late). He got fed up with it quickly, anxious to try his hand at less stickily romantic backgrounds, less sentimental themes. But always there were these damned reviewers, nostalgically and forever harking back to the early days. And publishers pointing to poor sales would insist on having more of the same. He would complicate and sophisticate his narrative manner with his growing mastery of technique, invent Marlowe ... tortuous and generally tiresome performances. How one does sympathize. Critics so cautious, so narrow, cretinous and even apparently malignant (it is not so; they are merely frightened of appearing foolish), force the writer into the groove where they have originally placed him. With rare and happy exceptions, reviewers are wretched.

There is an important and far-reaching difference between the young Conrad's experience in the literary world, and my own a half-century and more later. His first publisher, Fisher Unwin, was notoriously tight-fisted, parted with the greatest difficulty from fifty pounds or even twenty. He would defend himself by saying that one of 'his' books would always be taken seriously by the literary establishment. One would be assured of long, sympathetic and on the whole kindly reviewing in many a long-winded journal. In these Victorian times there were not as many dailies (the gutter press came to life only with the Boer War) but there was many a weekly, monthly, quarterly with a considerable readership and many columns to spare upon literary talent old and new. Thus, Mr Conrad, you don't get much money; you do get a lot of warm and even flaming write-up. By 1960 things had changed a good deal. This traditional reviewing space had disappeared or was like *Punch* on its last legs, found only in dentists' waiting-rooms. A couple of heavyweight gurus faced each other in the Sunday broadsheets; the bourgeois dailies pronounced upon the memoirs of generals; beneath a ponderous half-page existed a little fiction-bin for half a dozen novelists; lower still was a snippet rubric with thirty words for each of the four or five suppliers of the week's crime ration, where gentlemen with facetious pseudonyms summed up the offerings in a snappy phrase. In the one or two remaining political weeklies there would be something a scrap better, often witty, for a publisher to print on the back of a jacket after scissoring out the snide bits. One hoped for something like 'fresh and stimulating'.

The journalists are not to blame. Ever since the war there had been the uneasy feeling that reading was not a very serious way of spending time; got in the way of weightier occupations; something one admitted to half-heartedly, and with a deprecating giggle. There was always a good deal of the attitude later openly acknowledged by Richard Nixon – 'The arts you know – left-wing – Jews – stay away.' You could really be seen, only, reading war memoirs. It is the more surprising (though not very) to remember that in England there was little television then. 'I do enjoy Agatha Christie.'

What is still called crime writing was a muddled rag-bag. The detective stories were still predominant. Critics (mediocrities padding out their income) harked back a great deal, with nostalgia for the so-called 'Golden Age' of the 1920s and '30s when this light reading was acceptable relaxation from demanding intellectual labours: the puzzle was important. A row of wooden skittles was set up in lieu of characters and you had to guess which one was the guilty party. The tone was chatty and terribly facetious: this whole genre was described in the giggly cliché 'whodunnit'. I have always felt an immense respect for Dorothy Sayers who, earning a colossal income from this amiable tripe put it away, to concentrate her gifts upon the life of Christ and translating Dante. There was also an American version, even more ponderous and humourless, and a variation upon two-penny-blood lines, with tough dialogue, hard-bitten private-eye protagonists, raped girls and faster blood-boltered narration. This was also (if queasily) admired.

And there was also, thanks be, Ray Chandler, who put the cat among the pigeons; the bewildered Brits in a fearful fluster. He had no real precursor (Dashiell Hammett is as stilted as the worst of Hemingway) and no real follower: Ross MacDonald wrote well and was surely the better man, but couldn't 'throw the hard high one' which so captivated literary England: crime writing was suddenly respectable and vastly admired, but nobody else was deemed worthy – this is accurate enough: nobody in the 1940s and '50s had so original and insistent a talent.

Publishers didn't really care very deeply. They had in principle one or two solid money-spinners on their general list. They looked for and encouraged a stable of detective stories because these sold well, at little cost, and propped up worthy souls who merited an audience but didn't really cover their cost.

Victor Gollancz in 1960 is a good and vivid example of the situation. An independent publisher of the most cranky, rumbustious and fiercely free-minded kind: a few still existed. Victor ('we've been sorry for Germans, sorry for Jews, sorry for Arabs – what next?') had never been afraid of unpopular causes; had run the Left-Wing Book Club, had published George Orwell. He could afford it, underpinned by big-selling writers; he cherished crime stories. He decided that I would be a shining light in this genre; the thought had never occurred to me. Least of all did it occur that once thus branded this frivolous tittery label would be impossible to shake off. Type-casting of this sort has advantages: security and prosperity. Crime fiction was commercial and was easy to market.

I felt happy: I liked Victor. We shared tastes, for cigars, opera and Otto Klemperer. I was also newly rich, for contracts arrived every week and even movie offers. It is perfectly simple with hindsight, to see what should have been done. One moves to London, acquires a house in a pleasant if unfashionable quarter, cultivates one's new and enthusiastic acquaintances, joins a few professional associations and a good club. One could then settle to a very pleasant career, writing a book each year and having it comfortably pushed by the pals, reviewing for the Literary Supplement and first-nighting at Covent Garden. One would send the children as day-boys to Westminster or the French Lycée. One would do in fact exactly as my uncle Eardley, the Doctor, had done with conspicuous success.

Notice that these are not castles in Spain. Any bank would have agreed to the mortgage and at the time in question the prices were not exorbitant. Instead of which I bolted. One is not Nancy's son for nothing. Here and now it appears transparent, the elements quite obvious. There were the genes, the wretched restless blood; it was not only being homosexual that set Mike's feet a-tap. There was the angry impulsive impatience; the total lack of judgment, the loathing of convention, of piety and the bedside manner; both Mike and I detested the Doctor. The wish to fly in the face of all that was prudent and sensible, and everything which is thought to be a good investment. The utter irresponsibility with money, to which I join a hatred of banks and the dread of ever being indebted to them; lifelong and irrepressible. Happy the writer, even a bad one, a Galsworthy or a Maugham, who is on comfortable terms with the Stock Exchange. Unhappy the writer who sees and blurts out, 'Look, the Emperor has no clothes on.'

As though all this wasn't enough one has to add the tales of childhood and adolescence, villainously traumatic. If I could have isolated 'The Tale of Anne D.', detaching all shadow of the small boy she dragged around ... A tremendous insecurity and inadequacy; he loathed Ireland even while learning to love it. Aged twelve he felt a traitor. Every other little boy of his age grew up burning to be old enough to take a share in the battles. At eighteen the boy ran to London fussing about call-up papers, but the war was over. My Davidson cousins were generous and welcoming but in their eyes I saw condemnation. It was not, to be sure, my fault, but in 1939 I had lost the right to be English. And like my cousin Erskine, I wasn't Irish either. England being what it is, even in 1960 the idea of Empire, of being a world power, was clung to long after reality elsewhere had cast out illusion. The friends I was now making were all ten years older than myself, had all their row of battle ribbons earned in the blitz, where not on foreign fields. I was no longer the Londoner I was born; I was no longer English. A man who liked my early books, a witty judge and a brilliant King's Counsel, offered to put me up for the Garrick. But I had already bolted.

I hadn't intended to mention my wife; she is Dutch. She

enjoyed, loved and understood England, was perfectly at home there. One should I think remember that in the years before England joined what was then called the Common Market, and long before the rule that citizens of any Community country were free to enjoy if they so wished the right of residence, work, professional occupation and of course Social Security in any other country of the Community, the English frontiers were very strictly guarded. When therefore this girl came, in the 1950s, to England with the purpose of marrying me, it was on a visitor's permit. She married me and we were given a paper to prove it. Being British by birth as well as parentage on both sides my status was unquestioned, but (required by politish police officials to report monthly to the local commissariat which muttered that the Home Office worried about situations of this sort) the question arose. By marriage, she was told, she had acquired the right to British citizenship. But this would mean renouncing her Dutch passport. No way: I was proud of her. We are dealing here with the most stubborn, stiff-necked and hard-headed people, I dare say, anywhere. This is the blood of William the Silent. The Home Office is not much like the Duke of Alva but will be inclined to stiffness. So much the worse for the Home Office: the police chose tactfully to collapse.

I do not know where the Freelings came from. I have ventured the guess that the first was among Dutch and North-German contingents present on the field of Waterloo. Literature as well as history tells us that the cannon of Napoleon's last romantic and picturesque charge were heard in the ballrooms of Brussels. That the Duke said 'damned close-run thing'. That perhaps the riff-raff of Blücher made the minute difference: in France they would forever mumble, 'If only we'd had Marshal Davoust there instead of that worthless coward'. I quite agree: if only 'I' had been in the place of the worthless coward 'me'. Did I even say 'one can never trust the English'? I bolted. There are a lot of bolters in a battle, on both sides, and I don't blame myself all that much. Now that I think of it, bolting to Holland is logical and consequent. I felt myself very Dutch.

I am asking myself a question, ignoring the heckler's interjection upon this threadbare rhetoric – 'And a silly answer you'll get'. Why have I written these few autobiographical pages in so humourless a manner? I am writing for my children. Three of them were alive at the time I am speaking of: they were too small to understand but feel themselves concerned. Nancy was often very funny; at other times not funny at all but the onlooker could find her antics uproarious. In her later years, as her children increasingly worked themselves loose of the paralysing shadow, they found her comic, often farcical, and she could laugh whole-heartedly at some outrage of her own. Neither in this light does her son escape from the pattern set. My children think me funny as well as finding me ridiculous. I am quick as a rule to agree. I must also find humour in this exceedingly po-faced discussion of my own silly doings.

Humour one can – must – find, even in tragedy; a famous example is Hardy's celebrated 'The President of the Immortals had finished his sport with Tess'. Conrad's splendidly black gallows humour illuminates the pages of *The Secret Agent* and Greene is a master of the same. Coming closer to my world are the songs, dry comic little tunes played on a penny whistle, which one finds in Brecht; how lovely they are. How absurd is futility. How irritated one gets with Hamlet wittering on and incapable of laughing at the rogue and peasant slave.

The human condition, every minute, turns on the minutest grain of sand; a singles final at Wimbledon or Roland Garros has been decided by a dubious line call. All that fame and honour, prestige (and so much money) brought to ruin in a fraction of a second and a millimetre. Is it cruel to laugh? Calling it 'the gods' will not take the bitterness out of the joke.

So – we decide for ourselves, because we have free will? We are the captains of our fate? Mostly only in bad melodrama, like Sydney Carton mounting the scaffold: tell that to Winnie Verloc. We can snigger at a great deal of psychology, the chat about compulsions and rigidities, but when personally concerned we mostly see the joke too late.

I laugh now exuberantly at the stages by which 'I' arrived at this house – here, in this village. Along the way were other little houses, in France, in England and in Holland – even at one moment again in Ireland. For the government there, in a comic and ingenious scheme of attracting foreign investment, decreed also that 'artists' could live there free of income tax; the idea was momentarily seductive but the locals were as always quick to turn this *naïveté* to their own advantage. The place was full of drunk movie directors planning masterpieces and I laid a solid base myself for future alcohol addiction.

The little house in Holland, in the north where it was cheap, and buying unhindered by a multitude of regulations that restricted housing in the western coastal regions to the natives ... I had a great deal of innocent pleasure from this. At last! – it might have been Walter there exulting; a house of his own at last. Fresh from the builder's hand, I could finish and furnish it in perfect harmony with my own illusions of freedom: I might have just escaped from the dreariest and most restrictive of communist regulations in Latvia. A wonderful toy and I enjoyed myself immensely. This of course was 'Ampthill Road' all over again: it lasted a scant two years before the next – obligatory – bolt took place, one step ahead of asphyxiation. (Poor Nancy, how much I have come to understand and to sympathize.) A Dutch editor was named to the post of curator to a museum (much interest and great potential to himself); offered me his beautiful flat in a historic building, 'protected monument' on the Catharijnensingel in Utrecht. I wanted something of my own. Irritated and penned in by the multiplicity of bureaucracy, which applies and very much so to the admirable educational system of the Netherlands, I was conducting warfare with teachers (three boys progressing from nursery to elementary school) and the France of my own early childhood was calling to me. I was still bemused by the illusion of the liberty-fraternity syndrome: oh well, like many more before me and even since. Illusions are wonderfully highly coloured. I was persuaded that the little house, so beautified (and so sensibly...) by my great good taste, could be sold at vast profit: I didn't even scrape up the price I had given. Nor, no doubt, did 'Ampthill Road'. What matter – onward.

A sad affair, being incompetent with money. 'You have your hands on thousands,' yells Pew at the pusillanimous buccaneers, 'and you hang back. Oh, if I had eyes!' Having no eye for what after all is an elementary skill, seen and met with among the most ordinary and everyday company, is discouraging; worse, it's humiliating. There are small children who can make a football obey them. There are dull people and tongue-tied, in whose hands a wounded and frightened bird will relax in confidence, and there are silly talkative women for whom a drooping moribund plant will thrive: everybody has a talent. One could be utterly stunted and deprived. Jenny Wren, whose 'back is bad and legs are queer', has brilliant fingers and we are unsurprised. She has great strength of character and shrewd judgment; we are unsurprised. Sloppy (he has no other name) is good at woodwork and becomes a brilliant cabinet-maker. But most unexpectedly he can also 'do the police in different voices' and we are surprised, though we shouldn't be. Ulrich, the mechanic who could make that boring old Volkswagen sing and think itself a Porsche, is a rare phenomenon but not unheard-of. The man who had an idea, simple but of genius, like the safety-pin or the zip fastener, might have become immensely wealthy. One hopes he did, though it is far more likely that some cunning little shyster screwed him out of it. But there are plenty of people, quite dim and with no outstanding human quality, who know how to make a lot of money.

Genes have something to do with this. Everybody has noticed that Jews, historically persecuted and forbidden to practise most trades, further much hampered by the strict rulings
of their own ethical beliefs, learned financial skills: one must
believe these were very often bred into bone, generation after
generation: they helped one another too – and looked after
poor Jews. Thus it is easy to notice that aristocratic families,
forgetting the skills and daring that won them a prominent
social position at their origins, often made a fetish of despis-
ing money. The land-owning class, secure in broad acres and
ownership often unquestioned since feudal times, made a
point of not allowing crude cash to dirty their hands. Sir
Leicester Dedlock was quite unaware of how far Mr
Tulkinghorn had burrowed into his affairs. Fellow's there for
that, and well paid for it. It is interesting to speculate on
what he might have done had he learned that his wife's
personal honour, and thus his own, were threatened. If he
had been told that this little attorney had been consistently
embezzling ten per cent of his income he might eventually
have been moved to do something; much annoyed at having
to be bothered. His behaviour to the ironmaster is sympto-
matic: a gentleman is bound to offer hospitality but he can
scarcely bear having the fellow in the house.

Nancy greatly disliked having anything at all to do with
money. 'My bank manager, my solicitor'; two willing, devoted and grovelling instruments. There isn't any money?
Very well, one did without. If some whatsit-share declared an
extra dividend she was delighted. Consciously, she had never
earned a penny in her life. When a literary agency sold a
children's book she had written and actually sent her a che-
que, she was enchanted: it was a present.

I have reason to believe that Walter's notorious financial
incompetence (he meddled now and then with shares, selling
something sound but dull to invest in a flashy outfit) was
more pernicious. He made play with Dedlock beliefs and
attitudes, and how could one blame him? Mercifully free of

equestrian snobberies (the need to have a good seat and light hands) he was emphatic about shopkeepers' bourgeois mentalities. Long before the U-joke popularized by the Mitfords, he would not allow talk about mirrors or notepaper. The gun-metal watch and the bootlace. One never queried a bill; one paid it, and at once. One broke bread. Never have I forgotten the humiliation of being told by an Irish schoolmaster that I had bad table manners; that one cut bread ... One always gave way: never never did one thrust oneself forward. One said indeed 'Sir' to any man older than oneself, of any walk in life. If others put one in the wrong then one was in the wrong. Manners meant accepting the most boorish and ill-informed of opinions rather than pushing forward one's own. Manners dictated that one should always, humbly and anonymously, accept the worst back seat. When, forty years later, I came to read Molly Keane's book entitled *Good Behaviour* I came reluctantly to admit just how damaging this infernal code of manners could be. My poor Walter – what a burden you laid upon your son. In passing I remark that journalists to this day imagine that the Edwardians talked about 'the gels'. They have not heard the word spoken. Nancy to her dying day talked about 'the gairls' – the true Edwardian drawl. In the 1930s she became a movie addict: this is also illustrative. Her favourite, seen six times, was a perfect piece of girlish romanticism; Leslie Howard (surely the name says everything about him) as the Scarlet Pimpernel. I do not think she would have been much moved by the perils threatening Lady Blakeney, but to be rescued from the wicked French by this elegantly languid English gentleman struck, plainly, a chord deep within her. A year later appeared a new and much more physical heart-throb: Paul Robeson in *Sanders of the River*. This magnificent figure, naked bar the loincloth, standing in the bow of his boat singing 'The River Song' (sad bosh but a stirring rhythm – I was taken several times and still know it by heart) swept her away utterly. To be sure he was both black and a famous

Communist, which must have struck several and perhaps discordant notes. But the physical presence ... it is said that Peggy Ashcroft, the beautiful, the very talented, extremely English Desdemona to his splendid Othello, was instantly in bed with him. I am not a bit surprised, and one does wonder whether the thought ever occurred to Nancy, poor woman.

Since she went to every Howard movie, the child often accompanying, I had my first glimpse, in the *Petrified Forest*, of Bogart unshaved with the shotgun across his knee, as Duke Mantee. Was that my first crime story? I can date, with accuracy, the first conscious idea of crime writing: that was ten years later; a far better and unsentimental piece of film-making, illuminated by the immense Louis Jouvet. This was *Quai des Orfevres*. The impression was upon a mind still childish, since in 1947 I was twenty, but beginning to understand adult realities. Jouvet's portrait of the miserable, underpaid, cynical police officer is unforgettable.

It would be nice to think of Walter as madly in love with Ginger Rogers. Surely her style would have suited him; sexy in the open innocent manner of the American thirties (like the girl who waited at the station for the Chattanooga Choo-Choo); so free a dancer, rhythmical, athletic: I cannot see him attracted by anything lascivious. But I have no memory at all of his ever going to the 'pictures'. I know nothing of any secret areas in his heart. Did anyone?

Yes, I know; I find it hard to tear myself away. Yes; rambling ... The local cinema was the Plaza, just across Northam Bridge. It had an organ which came up out of the floor and changed colour while playing, and a theatrical little fellow who pulled out stops on a vast semicircular console.

For experience has shown me that in physical courage the boy was quite well endowed. But moral courage is something else. Plagued by hesitations and indecisions. What Americans used to call 'milquetoast'. How often haven't I thought, 'that was cowardly'. What the little Scotch boy called 'an awful jessie-like thing to do'. (He was being asked to

present a bunch of flowers to Lady Something, which of-
fended his sense of maleness; childhood example of moral
courage.)

The houses have all been lairs, hiding places where one
could lick wounds before coming out to show a brave face in
public. The very first was a boat which the young man
bought with the bit of money Walter left him; and promptly
lost. A boat for living in (a good one too) but most of all for
running away on.

At last there would be this house. I must describe the
village; cruising in circles, to look from every viewpoint. I
must then land at a specific point. Wings folded, I enter the
lair.

PART TWO

The Village

THIS VILLAGE IS IN THE VOSGES, a range of lowish, eroded mountains in eastern France. The bird characteristic of this landscape is the buzzard; he is always present. One sees him high up, travelling in lazy swirls, indifferent to us, busy ants below. The immense view has little interest for him. His business is with thermals, the veer of air currents: we may suppose he studies wind and rain. Down he comes, a fluid spiral. His pass at ground level is decisive as the new-honed scythe with which men, now old, mowed these steep meadows. Who keeps count of the mice? God, perhaps.

The bird sits on a sagging fencepost. I walk slowly; almost I can touch him. His eye, mild and magnificent like Browning's Lost Leader's, shows contempt; he slides off effortless. I am earthbound, clumsy and foolish. He is the historian, the geographer, anatomist and sociologist.

I have tried to learn from him, to give my loutish approach a scrap of his grace. His objectivity; this land is mine but how much more is it his. I mimic his methods. I am trying to look at this old, scarred, European land as he would, through his aerial perspective. I cannot see as he does. In westerly weather the cloud can cling to these hillsides for days: at times the valley fills with mist. I can hear, smell, even touch, but am blind. But when the easterly blows, from Russia across central Europe – then, like the Kaiser's surveyor (to be met within these pages), I stand on this mountain named the Donon, I can look, it seems to me then, so clear is the air, so limitless the view, far. That geometer planted here a bronze compass rose. An arrow points, the lettering says 'Saint Petersburg'. Face around, turn about and another will say 'Madrid'. Midway, this is my Europe.

I am here alone; at the end of his life Proust was alone with his book.

I wished then to spiral down, like the hawk (but he is not interested in men). To shorten and narrow the perspective, to ground, house, man level. It will be frustrating to read over what I write (cramped and flabby pedantries). But by devious ways – and I propose also to look at these – God who did not choose that I should be a hawk set me down here. I was an Englishman parachuted here – as in wartime were others, whose graves are marked, in these woods. But I was not told to bring comfort to partisans, an assurance of help coming; I was only told to live here and to look around me. And, since I am a writer, to dip the finger into ink. 'Write it down.' I have tried to obey. Here are the hills of the Vosges, and here is the village.

It is, in part, the story of a little-known region of France, and that is an interesting land, nexus of our European peninsula, our near-island. France is extremely varied, and much of it – even today – beautiful, so that much has been written about it; sometimes well and more often vulgarly, ignobly. Little enough has been written about these, the eastern marches which border upon the Low- or Netherlands, upon Germany, upon Switzerland. A section of this book is bound thus to have a tediously didactic flavour. The English people have sometimes felt themselves concerned with it, but rarely and then in a militaristic sense: the wars of the Duke of Marlborough; the Somme in 1916; the trenches of Flanders in that great and terrible wartime; the breakthrough in 1944 from Normandy to the marches of Holland. That is one reason; another is that this is not really 'France' at all: it is the Rhineland, a totally different concept. I have attempted to make this clearer.

It is also the tale of an attraction; physical, magnetic. Genetics as a science is now understood, or so we are told. The why and wherefore of inherited characteristics remains obscure and explains the fascination everyone feels about origins. Where did I come from and what, there, contributed to shaping me? – this is a universal question. The moment we are self-conscious enough to assemble any facts about parentage, we will begin to wonder whether environment will also exercise a genetic effect, modifying inherited, atavistic instincts. After three generations as village blacksmith the trade is in the blood and so is the village. Or as Kipling noticed after buying his house, it didn't matter who held the title deeds: 'Old man Hobden owns the land'. I am myself well aware of the wandering vagabondage strong in my own inheritance. Was it only a series of trivial coincidences that brought me to this village? Why have I stayed here for over thirty years?

Part of this tale is about self-discovery: to what shores are we voyaging? In this sense, here is also a travel book. Journeying, it is evident, is through time as well as space; physics, and also metaphysics. We stand still, and we hurtle; village, continent, entire planet. To be bound upon the wheel, and to seek to be free of it; that is a very old and universal quest.

The village itself has changed, profoundly and often laughably, in the 'only' thirty years I have lived here. To begin to understand I must start with the past. With physical geography, changing little, and with history, in constant flux.

Freelings, obeying heaven knows what instinct, have always been bolters. Nearly two hundred years ago one bolted into England, and since then into every other corner of the globe. I know myself to be a European, and betimes tell myself that we have completed our given pattern. That I have come home.

2

GEOGRAPHY

I MUST BEGIN with the mountains. We need a map. Any good atlas will do. *The Times Atlas*, plate 69, 'France North-East'. This gives us our bearings. Paris on the left, fringes of England at the top, the Rhine all the way down the right and a glimpse of Switzerland at the bottom. This map does not show Holland, the estuaries of the great rivers, but here between Rhine and Maas (in French named Meuse, as we say 'Rhine') is my subject; my home.

The appellation 'Rhineland' is generally used as applying only to the German bank, and then only to that part of it between the confluence of the Mosel/Moselle (whose upper reaches are Lorraine, and thus French) and the frontier of Holland. Obviously, the Rhineland must include both banks. The confused nomenclature betrays centuries of nationalist rivalry, as odious as it is ridiculous.

We will do better to remember that Lorraine is only the French for Lotharingia; that Lothar or Louis was Charlemagne's son. The great-Charles, who ruled over most of Western Europe, divided his empire into three slices for his three sons, in an effort to be fair. We would say ill-advisedly, but all of history is ill-advised.

The Times Atlas is comprehensive and meticulous, but does not name Grandfontaine. Reasonably; a small and obscure village. It does mark the mountain named the Donon, and the pass through the Vosges called the Col du Donon. Both lie within the territory of our commune: 48.30 north latitude, almost exactly; a fraction east of 7 degrees east longitude. In geography, and in history, on the line of march between Strasbourg (important river passage) and Paris. The Celts came this way. We will agree: in European history a very important detail. Here they crossed the Vosges. In front of them lay the wonderful, rich and fertile land of France. They went on into the Abendland, the sunset land, of Finisterre at the end of the European peninsula; into Galicia in Spain; into the harsh granite plateau of Bretagne; flooded over into Cornwall and Wales, north and west into Scotland and Ireland. That is not at this minute my interest. A lot of them stayed here hanging about. Perhaps they were tired by the long trek up the Danube valley. Perhaps they got this far and thought, the hell with it. The Donon, here, became for them a sacred mountain, a place of great symbolic importance.

They remained and grew strong. Caesar, great Roman general, tearing through Gaul like a dose of salts, used always his immense political skill, tactically as well as strategically (a very good general). These peoples, Celt or Germanic ('Gaul' is an extremely vague concept), were forever quarrelling with one another. He didn't so much *veni vidi vici* as most skilfully set them at odds. Divide and conquer, what. Thereafter, tactically, Roman discipline did the trick. Hereabouts, in these damned twisty mountain defiles, there was a lot of trouble.

Tacitus has some mention. 'Germans' and 'Celts' get muddled. A tiresome priestess called Velleda (she has left her traces hereabouts) did much to unify quarrelling tribes. Be this as it may, Roman rule became very firm around here. This all belongs to the following chapter, but the geography becomes history instantly: we'll be back among these Romans.

For the Vosges form a natural barrier, dividing the Rhine valley of which the French bank is called Alsace from Lorraine and from Bourgogne. The roads through this barrier are crooked and difficult. The pass of the Donon is relatively direct. The only other easy passage is the col de Saverne, chosen by nineteenth-century engineers to carry the railway, and in our days the autoroute. It has easier gradients but lies northward, making a big loop in the direct road. The Donon was less of a trudge. We can be grateful that most modern traffic avoids it. Only the airlines take this path still, and their pollution is dissipated in the upper air.

Romans always cast a long shadow across history. Napoleon admired them greatly and when he cut up France for administrative purposes into a hundred-odd *départements* (each to be ruled by a Prefect) this potty village formed the junction of four of them. Both in geography and in history this is a nerve centre, a strategic spot. Grandfontaine is defensible against the west, and in 1914 under German occupation was so defended. It was also defended in the centuries-long surge of peoples from the east – from beyond the Elbe.

Mountains: geologically the Vosges are very old, outlines worn and softened by aeons of erosion, rounded and wooded almost to the summits. There is no perpetual snow; they are not impressive, as Alps are. From that plane, over our heads, they would appear as a tumbled, muddled belt of forest with rocky outcrops. But this is among the boredoms of flying, that it crushes the earth we walk on. Victorians thought Alps 'sublime', but so also was Golden Cap or Eggardon. Or Ditchling Beacon. The Donon – a little hill – is the height of Snowdon. Seen from Strasbourg, across the Alsace plain, the Vosges look picturesque but nowise formidable until your feet bring you to the nursery slopes where the vines grow, and you see them above you, and learn to measure these hills by the height of your boots.

The chain runs roughly north and south. North from the Gap of Belfort (beyond which lies the Jura, and behind that the Alps) are the Ballons, great sprawling massifs two thousand metres high. In reality – my imagination exaggerates – twelve hundred and getting steadily lower northward until, past Saverne, they peter out into gentle hills, green valleys, and the Palatinate. The Donon is the last of the real mountain massifs.

They are still formidable; writhed and knotted: there is

always another little col to pass, another steep little valley, another village masked from view. Delays and hindrances multiply. It is a landscape of much beauty; rainclouds part suddenly, allowing unexpected and spectacular vistas. Officially this is only the most widespread woodland of Europe. Betimes, still primitive forest. It is easy to get lost here when walking. It is possible to die here. Medically of exhaustion, exposure. I should insist, of fear, of terror. These woods are silent, haunted by many spirits and by no means all of them beneficent. Sunny, happy woods; within a breath sinister and malevolent; I have walked much in them. Even on the roads, and in a car, it does not do to be in a hurry.

It is a sandstone land; fresh-chipped, of a brilliant carmine. Weathered, of a delicate greyish-pink. Dirty, as in all the urban architecture hereabout, lees of wine. As a building stone, free-working and of classical beauty; a little over-soft. These hills are also mineral-rich, and everywhere quarried and delved. The mines of Grandfontaine – as will be seen – are not the least interesting. In this harmonious, balanced landscape, so reminiscent of Chinese (and Japanese) painting, the two essential components of every classical composition are always present; the woods, the water.

Rivers. Our climate shows this sense of balance. The northerly wind funnels down from the Pole; it is not rare; it is profoundly unpleasant. Our southerly is a summer phenomenon; hints of orange and oleander – and desert too. The easterly reminds us that this is central Europe, an extravagance of both cold and heat. But our prevailing wind is the Atlantic westerly. When the battle fleet of dark majestic cumulus rides up, Nelsonian in line astern, it rains here as in Finisterre. Grandfontaine the well-named lies on the easterly brink of the watershed: our streams flow east to feed the Rhine, and from outside my front door I could paddle a canoe unchecked to Rotterdam. But the sheltering forest protects us from the storm-wind.

A condor sees this region as the birthplace of great rivers.

From here Seine and Marne flow westward, to water the Ile-de-France. Northward runs the Meuse, to become the Maas in Belgian Liege, and northeasterly through many steep rocky gorges the Moselle will become Mosel and join the Rhine in Germany. They have all Vosgean origins. On the Donon itself rises the Saar, to flow north and join the Mosel at Trier, a great Roman fortress, and we understand why.

Europe is very small. Fernand Braudel, far-sighted historian, described it as the *presqu'île*, the near-island. Here in Grandfontaine ('the big source') one will grasp this clearly. Our tiny rain-fed brooks, uncountably many, form a nexus, spreading into little rivers, life-blood of the region. These turn, join, into a spiderweb of waterways which make a nonsense of the old nationalist frontiers.

Myself, I would have to journey to the end of the Vosges, at the Belfort gap, where Alsace becomes the Franche Comté, to find rivers flowing south, towards the sea that divides Europe from Africa. That is not my purpose. Nor do I more than notice that a very short way eastwards, in the Schwarzwald which is not in the least a black forest in cherry-blossom time, I would find myself standing at the source of the Danube, and that to say the least is another story. My concern, and my home, is the Rhineland. (One might notice that both Rhine and Danube have their source within a minute distance.)

Indeed Claudio Magris, another historian of European humanism, describes the difference as being no more than the two slopes of a house's roof. The portage ways between the great rivers are everywhere small. Reaching Paris, by way of the Marne valley, it is no great matter to join the westward-flowing Loire at Orleans. Nomadic peoples could – did – travel thus from the Black Sea to the Atlantic. The twisted, knotted Vosges barrier is the only real obstacle along this mighty journey. They crossed the Rhine at Strasbourg (name meaning the crossroads city) and they paused here on the Donon, shading their eyes against the westering sun, before

they plodded on into the Abendland, sunset land, of the nar-
rowing peninsula.

The Rhineland is my concern and my passion, for it is my
home. The water tastes the same, since it is the same. Of
what use to us are these idiotic frontiers put up by politicians?
We are knocking them down at last. Here, in Lotharingia, we
understand each other very well. It is said, there is a language
barrier. We have learned from birth – it is said – to speak
French, German, or Dutch. The people, the Volk, have always
spoken a Germanic dialect, a plattdeutsch which in essentials
varies little from the Schwyzerdutsch where the Rhine rises
on the Swiss frontier, through the many variations of
Alsacien, through Luxemburg and Flanders, on to the Dutch
of the estuaries. This language is like the Yiddish of
European Jews; it has regional accents, local words culled
from the preponderating literary languages. It unifies. A Jew
in Prague, Bialystok or Belgrade had no trouble in Brussels.
Speaking patois, the Rhinelanders make themselves understood and that is often more than we can manage.

Chesterton remarked that all English roads were made by
drunks on the way home from the pub, a fact true anywhere.
In the pub flourish those quarrels about disputed bits of
land, dear to country people. In Alsace, a farmland thickly
peopled, the next village is visible across the fields but the
road zags and zigs for twice as far as the crow flies since
litigation clings to every boundary stone and nobody talks to
those foreigners in the next village. But once in the Vosges,
where farms are smaller and the people fewer, since much of
the land is forest, the pig went to market by the easiest route,
and that was to follow the rivers.

West of Strasbourg, crossing the Alsace plain, the Vosges
stretch in front of one, an irregular but solid line of horizon-
blue. Closer, foothills; the vineland, source of wealth. Many
prosperous and picturesque little towns. Some are still
walled, with massive fortified gateways, and a few pages
further I will try to show why. For now the road to

Grandfontaine swings with the river, turning around the higher, darker and more forbidding hills beyond. Into increasingly narrow defiles as one begins to climb the Donon massif. Villages straggle; smaller, sparser. They have still Germanic names. Grandfontaine, the last village of Alsace, is the first to have a French name, announcing the pass, and Lorraine beyond. This settlement – at first sight uninteresting – is the link between the two provinces. Germany is left behind, and France is in front of us.

At the foot of the Donon the little river turns abruptly south – smaller as it nears the sources. Here our own hill stream runs down to meet and swell it. At Strasbourg it will meet in turn the Ill – and a mile or so further, the Rhine. Some of these Vosges valleys are wide and sunny; south-facing sunny uplands, famous for pear and cherry; vines will not flourish this high. Some are dark and damp; the trees grow stiffly, up rocky steeps, and frown at one. A road will turn, seeming without end, between woods close crowded to the verges, grim and hostile, not a house to be seen. A little pass is marked by the ubiquitous sign put there by Michelin, but in the gap may be the crouching ruin of a little castle. Medieval robber-barons who were not in the least picturesque.

This is the forest land, where woodcutters' children lost their way and were captured by witches. In sunlight it is magical, in rain an enchantment of moss and fern; at night sinister and also extremely frightening. One can at any moment get lost, easily, alarmingly; and then one must follow water downhill . . .

The characteristic, indeed predominant tree of the Vosges is a conifer; tall, columnar, close ranked, giving the forest its dark Gothic look, and the French call it simply *sapin*. In the south so it is; *Abies alba*. My pompous botanizing can be forgiven, since by some obscure choice of its own, in the northern Vosges another tree altogether is the most frequent; *Picea abies* (the Norway spruce). But both are fine forest trees with similar habits, undeterred by steep ravines or draughty heights. I put in a claim for liking the spruce better. Fluid, fan-shaped swags of foliage swing from the curved branch like the folds of a theatre curtain. One looks up a narrow defile; it's a classical Hokusai painting. Seen from below, sunlight filtering between; a noble vision.

It is by no means all a black forest. A lot of it is beech. In springtime those clear pale greens marry happily with the emerald sparks of new growth on the conifers. And in autumn when the firs are saddest on some cloud-besieged hill, the russet haze gladdens our eye. Up the road here is a beech hanger on a nigh vertical-seeming rock wall. The sun gives dark stone and pale tree a stagy glitter; exhilarating.

We've other trees too; since the more seldom the more noticeable, and generally in the open; oak (and the scarlet oak, though I'm not sure it's a native), Spanish chestnut, birch and rowan and wild cherry; near villages ash, and by waterways aspen and willow. The State foresters experiment with replanting; fire is no very great hazard in this damp temperate woodland, though in a dry summer ... Much of the forest is intensively and brutally harvested.

Patrick Leigh Fermor says somewhere that the cypress is civilized but the spruce betokens barbarism. The great man must have had a drink too many on some red-hot Greek hillside; that is sentimental nonsense. The Mediterranean shores were deforested for shipbuilding and goats did the rest. Efforts to rejuvenate are condemned by fire; by the hideous careless hatred of mankind; by concrete, and by the corruption that allows the concrete to flow. A tree some centuries old is sawn because it interrupted a rich man's view. The Greek light, the Phos which illuminated the obscurity of our souls, is not what it was. We must go north now, for succour.

Man cannot progress towards civilization without trees and without water. The basic equation is that the tree retains the soil and holds the moisture. The tree oxygenates the air while absorbing the viler gases. Is it a secondary consideration that the tree is noble and beautiful, while the automobile is ugly and base? I must not talk about the Amazon or Indonesia. A European, I love the cypress and the spruce. Everyone knows that the car and the truck, displacing the donkey and the bicycle, destroyed the shore. That the fragile inland seas cannot resist the chemical and bacteriological onslaught. Any more than the outboard motor. And the forest, we may think, won't last much longer either.

To my generation (what is left of it) the forest lay altogether outside the known world. Indeed the village, thirty-five years ago – it betrays my age to think of this as a short time – had changed little in a century. This house lay on its outskirts and the forest pressed close upon us. Animals at night rambled freely around it: deer came down to drink, foxes and martens were often seen and met with, and a polecat nested in the roofspace. The forest was full of wood and water spirits and could often be terrifying. I am aware that I have been a timid, solitary, imaginative child, brought up among and upon books, but there is nothing the least unusual about that. There was no television, cars and phones were rarities (even in town we had only recently got accustomed to all three) and electricity itself was uncertain in rural Europe, a primitive spirit itself, at the mercy of winter snowfall or summer thunderstorm. Nor was there much noise. The odd tractor rumbled past, the odd plane droned overhead. I am saying that the air, the water, the soil itself, were still largely free of the pollution which now presses so heavily and mortally upon us.

I would have to drive the children back to their schools, to the town. Sometimes my wife would do this. Or sometimes she would keep the car and I would come out here on a bicycle, to work for a few days in quiet, alone, in the silence. I walked then much, in the woods, and often by myself. On still, sunny afternoons the trees, grave and gothic, would begin quite quietly to move, and then one had to beware. Or in deep silvered winters, behind the curtain of stalactites masking a fissure in rock, there were voices which the ear did not quite catch. Under ice trees groan, and make sudden loud complaint. Betimes one has to push oneself, to banish the fiend that close behind does tread. There are incantations which help; Shakespeare lyrics or the gallows poems of François Villon. Or '*Quand vous serez bien vieille, au soir, à la chandelle*' ... Or John Donne.

Perhaps Professor Tolkien is now seen as a harmless old blitherer, dwarves and hobbits for small children. Not to my generation. The pipes and beer, hearty rambles to Oxfordshire pubs, are tedious, and tiresomely twee; he knew nothing about women: notwithstanding, I do not think he was right to suggest that some trees have a bad character. They are not like human beings: they aren't concerned with our struggle between good and evil. The Ents were a brilliant concept, but I don't accept the anthropomorphic suggestion that they take vengeance upon the malefactor.

Certainly though, they fear and dislike mankind, their worst enemy. They collect and project man's fear of Pan. Certainly, living on the frontier between men and trees, here, has taught me much. Auden, a poet older than me but not much, has a terrifying line about the woods which come up, and stand around, 'in deadly crescent'. They do here now, around me, around my meadow which surrounds the garden, at a bare hundred metres' distance. They form an amphitheatre of classical beauty. They do not threaten me. Malevolence is in ourselves.

The reality of the forest is metaphysical. Reason is not much help. Chemistry, biology – or meteorology – tell us that the woodlands are precious. Ecology, that they are fragile, vulnerable. Materialism sees only a source of income. Instinct, and emotion, becomes too readily sentimental; little Paul, asking what the waves were always saying. He was right, though: what are we drinking, the water or the wave? Essence and existence continue to put questions to which we have no answer.

Rock and rain, wood and water, intermingling in harmony like a string quartet. A banal image, and one which could apply to many regions of Europe which illustrate the self-containment as well as the continuity. To isolate this small area is impossible, since it knits together in ways long thought politically unacceptable. The purpose of this little didactic exercise has only been to demonstrate that the Vosges land is not 'part of France', as was for some centuries taught and maintained, but an integral part of the Rhineland. Geographically this is so; I can show that this is also a historical truth.

3

The History

WE KNOW LITTLE ENOUGH about pre-Christian Europe. I have no more idea about what the French call *nos ancêtres les Gaulois* than have the French; a lot of myth and misinformation, and not much fact. Handbooks of prehistory centre upon archaeological finds.

From these are traced the progress up the Danube valley of Celts; an evolved people, of great talent. Others were here before them, and subsequent arrivals of other peoples out of the east make the palimpsest nigh unreadable. The need or instinct always to press on further, towards the Abendland, into the sunset, meant that the Celts gathered on the western fringes of the peninsula: they are still there. Did some stop and settle along the way – here for instance? We know nothing much before the Roman historians, priggishly pleased with themselves. Other peoples are barbarians. Where has one heard such sentiments already? My own generation, last of empire-building Brits, was stuffed with this at school.

Thus Livy has a lot to say about Celts storming down into Italy, giving the nascent Roman Republic a nasty fright. One gets to know little about Etruscans, more civilized but less bellicose. As for the Rhineland, we know nothing definite before Caesar's campaigns in Gaul, and then Tacitus (much of whom is lost). Some mumbling about Nervii and Batavii, a tough lot but this is only military materialism. The same as across the Channel – ancient Britons – and one knows no more than the rumours in Herodotus.

Celts followed the natural path, up the Danube valley. There seems always to have been an easy passage of the Rhine at or near Strasbourg. The river formed sandbanks and perhaps there were islets which would have made fording more feasible. Strasbourg itself is a very ancient settlement. Romans would fortify it, call it Argentoratum and keep a garrison there, obviously to guard the river passage. A few centuries on, Gibbon tells of a large and extremely menacing 'barbarian' invasion at this point. In one of the last great feats of Roman arms the Emperor Julian gathered the garrisons of the Vosges (this would have included the Donon encampment), came storming down from Saverne with a very small army, and threw the villains back across the Rhine with great losses, there to lick their wounds and keep quiet for a goodish while: the Battle of Strasbourg is important. Perhaps a lot got drowned? I do not know when the first bridge was built. Not, I should think, before medieval times and then a wooden structure easily burned when not swept off by the Rhine flooding with the yearly snowmelt.

Guesswork: the Donon may have been a sacred mountain beforehand. Certainly it was so to Celts. There must have been another – and material – reason for its importance. This was, I should think, the iron mines of Grandfontaine, of which I shall have plenty to say, since their importance persists into this century. The ore has a tungsten element, so that it became especially sought-after for weaponry, until the invention of steel. Celts were considerable metallurgists, and it is fair to suppose that they worked these mines.

Romans thought so too. The Vosges are rich in minerals. Only a step southward is the area now known as Sainte-Marie-aux-Mines, worked by the Roman administration for silver, lead, jewels, besides iron. All sorts of goodies. But as Kipling saw and learned in Sussex, the iron of Grandfontaine had a military value.

For Celts, and for other native peoples, the Donon had a mystic significance. To our sorrow, the worship and rituals are obscured. There was a temple there, a sanctuary. But when excavated in the nineteenth century this was recognizably of Gallo-Roman gods. The French have always been content with this. Rome to them has always been the basis of known civilization. Just so, propaganda down to our own days has insisted that Germanic peoples were (are) barbarous savages and thus of no interest. We are immeasurably the poorer for this imbecile dogma.

The frontier fortress of Argentoratum was of enormous importance. Augustus had his triumphs in the north. Trier and Köln (Cologne) became tremendous bastions. Roman arms advanced through much of waterlogged Holland, up as far as Scotland ... Strasbourg, the crossroads town, became the base for Roman rule all along the Danube line, up to Dacia and the Black Sea. For some hundreds of years the Donon was an important link in this empire-building: the garrison there formed part of a mobile reserve; the mine, we may guess, a valuable source of revenue. Traces subsist; a Roman road still visible runs north to Boulay in Lorraine, supply route to Trier and the northern strongholds. All this feeds the legend that the left bank of the Rhine was a frontier, defending the imperium from barbarism. The notion has persisted to our own days.

Roman piety, obliterating local religious ceremonial or, what is politically more skilful, adapting sanctuaries to their own forms of worship, left the Donon unrecognizable. Tacitus mentions a Celtic priestess hereabout, focus of local discontent and rebellion, but we are left with the might-have-been. Just so, in future years, Christians would take pains to build churches on sites of pagan worship. In Brittany zealous pastors encouraged the demolition of menhirs. Here also, the site was plundered for building-stone. Other – and interesting – edifices used massive cut blocks which by tradition 'came from the Donon'; dams, reservoirs, canalizations – so that we will never know. On the summit today is a fake temple in the sentimental nineteenth century style, a few casts of Gallo-Roman statuary, and a few blurred traces on which tourists scratch their names.

Dark Ages; they are as black here as anywhere, and as obscure. No doubt as beastly too; perhaps we were more fortunate than most. This borderland, poor, obscure, and difficult of access, escaped much of the torment which is all we generally know of medieval centuries. Westward the great magnates, Dukes of Lorraine and of Burgundy, disputed ownership of enormous provinces: this hilly woodland strip was of no great interest, probably because it didn't produce much money and taxes were difficult to collect. Eastward Strasbourg was a free imperial city, wealthy and prosperous, owing allegiance to the Prince-Bishop, who also had a very sharp eye to the taxes. Around here areas of woodland are to this day known as 'the Bishop's'. Grandfontaine one would think must have been rather a plum because of the mines, but they seem to have fallen into disuse during much of this time. Along the line of the Vosges many petty war-lords built castles, played the robber-baron to anyone who came along, made life a misery to the local peasantry. Many can still be seen, in a generalized state of ruin but attesting to illiterate and ferocious exactions. Along the line of the foothills greater lords like the Counts of Andlau cultivated their vines, were a lot richer, and thus a lot more civilized.

It is possible that enclaves of relative peace were due to church ownership. Close to us, the Benedictine monasteries of Senones and Marmoutier held much land. A heavy-handed ownership no doubt, but preferable to the more rapacious barons. To their archives we owe some information, but mostly of later date, when a small princedom of Salm claimed ownership over these lands and dickered with the Duke of Lorraine over the rights to minerals.

Down in Alsace, and in the Schwartzwald on the other bank – all along indeed both banks of the Rhine – war and destruction raged perpetually. We can read horrible stories of Jews plundered and burned, people chopped or broken on the wheel on scaffolds, every appalling barbarity in every little town. With the Wars of Religion things get steadily worse. All of this land – it is so to this day – is half Catholic and half Protestant, and each massacred the other with holy zeal.

Culminating perhaps with the Swedish armies. *Les Suèdois*
are still a bogy with which children are frightened.

The fortified towns of the foothills before referred to,
Mutzig and Rosheim protecting the river gap, protected us.
Armies, be they Catholic or Protestant, stayed mostly in the
lowlands. It is probable again that the wooded highlands af-
forded poor pickings. Our little local market town, at the foot
of the Donon where the Bruche valley turns south, is
Schirmeck. The little towns thereafter Saales, and Saint-Dié
and Epinal, become steadily more French: this is the last, on
the roads westward, to have a Germanic name. We have
made jokes; *Schirm-Eck*, the Umbrella Corner. It is likely
though that this was truly named the Place of Refuge.

History here, for a couple of hundred years, is the story of
the rivalry – the hatred – between the Most Catholic King and
the Most Christian King. Which sounds immensely funny.

Marie de Bourgogne, the great heiress, married a
Habsburg. The result was that Charles V, King of Spain,
Holy Roman Emperor, owned all of Germany, Austria, and
the Netherlands, most of Italy, and most of what is now eastern France: besides Spain, the New World, and various odd
corners, like islands. Poor little France felt very hard done by,
having gone to all the trouble of getting rid of Great Dukes,
not to speak of the English. Still, France possessed a powerful secret weapon: Cardinal Richelieu, himself immensely
Catholic, was very good friends with both Protestants and
Turks, horrible infidels whom he felt sure would give no end
of trouble to Charles' rather less competent successors (he
was quite right). Cardinal Mazarin continued these policies
but it took a long long time to clear the Spanish out of
present-day France. Condé and Turenne were such good generals that the war was carried into Germany; their successors
were less talented. The Duke of Marlborough and Prince
Eugene had the better of later developments. Alsace, and the
Vosges, were hideously shuttlecocked between all these martial blood drinkers. When I first came to Grandfontaine I got

a bad fright; a farm just down the road is named Malplaquet. 'Can't possibly be the same one...' but it took some hasty thinking.

There are a lot of Protestants in Alsace: to this day the two religions are evenly balanced. To the credit of the University of Strasbourg must go the fact that this is the only place to have two faculties of theology, side by side in holy harmony.

After Picardie and Artois to the north, and the Franche Comté to the south, Alsace became French. A beautiful set of engravings shows Louis XV entering his lovely new province, with much pomp. There was a huge triumphalist party, at colossal expense, in the loyal and faithful city of Strasbourg.

Two consequences are immediately apparent. First is that France has again, as in Roman times, a frontier on the Rhine, where she has no business. The two banks are or should be identical in custom, manner and politics; their religion is likewise their own affair. If there has to be a frontier then it comes right here, in Grandfontaine and along the crests of the Vosges. Only now are we beginning to admit and understand this fact.

The second is that Alsace was not happy to be told it was French – and to a large degree still isn't. A nostalgia lingers for the 'free imperial city'; almost one would say for the Prince-Bishop, when Alsace got on with its affairs without a lot of meddling from Berlin or Vienna, but especially from Paris. Being independently bloody-minded is still a strong trait in this people. One cannot tell what traces might subsist of Goth and Hun and Vandal and all the others, but it is markedly a Germanic Volk, uneasy within that solid-seeming French Hexagon. Exactly like the Basque land which happens to lie on the French side of the Pyrenees.

Throughout the eighteenth century, Grandfontaine made itself exceedingly small. The heavy-handed centralized administration of Paris would not have been greatly noticed here: this was still the Princedom of Salm. A few roads, some rather heavier taxes. A lick of French taste and sophistication, interest in the arts, would scarcely touch the village. Uncouth barons built elegant and delicious palaces of the lovely red stone, in Senones and Saverne and of course in Strasbourg. Poorer people pushed further into the highlands, clearing woods and dry-walling with the stones in this thin soil. These little upland farms are no longer to be seen but the walls are still to be found beneath woodland undergrowth.

Only another few years and in a respectable town house on the Place Broglie in Strasbourg (it is now the Banque de France) a young man edified assembled notables by singing them the Song of the Rhine Army, full of chauvinist jingo sentiment. Rousing tune; luckily nobody knows the words. The pious prayer that our fields be watered with the impure blood (sic) is even more deplorable than other national anthems: a few months more and Napoleon flashed across, on his way to Ulm and Wien and Berlin. This Empire, as grotesque and short-lived as Hitler's, a little less lunatic, a lot less wicked, was peacefully settled, surely a tribute to the civilized eighteenth-century mind. France kept the frontiers of before the revolution, including Alsace. The Rhine would know another fifty years of peace.

With the nineteenth century I will be proposing to look at this in close detail – Grandfontaine enters a time of importance; for a few, of wealth and prosperity; a time of industrial development, of the Forges. Some of the traces left by this are still visible. Following close upon it came our greatest political upheaval. This left fewer physical traces. The kindly woods have come close to obliterating them. But upon the minds of men the stamp was heavier. 'Nationalism' was and is a horrible concept. Living here, I have a better understanding of fires not yet quenched, as in Northern Ireland.

The French administration of the mid-nineteenth century was no worse than any other. Solid, orderly, bureaucratic. The lordly, pretty palaces on the Place Broglie became the Town Hall, and the Prefecture of the Bas-Rhin, harmlessly enough. But to ensure the grip of government, on both banks of the Rhine, the nationalist spirit was fomented, encouraged, provoked, irritated. Bismarck was unifying Germany, as the Republic had unified France. A mood of martial braggadocio predominated. Small pretexts were seized upon to make certain the war of 1870. In Paris they screamed 'Forward to Berlin' and over there it was 'Forward to Paris'.

We know what happened. The Kaiser, delighted, captured Alsace; when all is said a province of Germanic culture and language (for once, religion had nothing to do with it). While the going was good he took most of Lorraine, the idea being to deprive France of industrial coal and iron, and weaken future military potential. The frontier was established here in the village, with the Donon as its corner-stone. Grandfontaine became German, which it had never been. Here two political nationalist cultures met and clashed hideously. Only now is this bitterness beginning to die away under the dead leaves.

The reality of two genuinely different cultures is – even today -apparent. On the eastern slope of the Donon ours is the only village to have a French name. Beyond, on the Lorraine *versant*, the villages are French; look different, and are. Within Alsace this is to this day referred to as 'The Interior'. France ... But propaganda, in Paris assiduously cultivated, still insists that everything is French, right up to the river's indifferent flow down towards the North Sea. What proportion of this water was Swiss? What Dutch? A cartographer in Paris, drawing maps of the artillery ranges for the War Office, insisted that *half* the water was French.

Of this chauvinist mentality I will give two illustrations. First my family doctor in Schirmeck. His name is German. Like his father and grandfather (it is a dynasty) he is the Doctor, a much-loved village notable. The grandfather – it is said – got up every morning and sang 'La Marseillaise' before breakfast. Punished rather mildly by the German authority with exile, for passing military information to 'the enemy'. While in a Lorraine village a little girl's grandfather, pointing to the Route de Metz, told her 'I will not live to see it, but you will see a French army march up that road.' And in 1918 she did. For fifty years the thought and the talk was of vengeance; of patriotism; of the need for Frenchness, and of the duty bound to hate the enemy.

When I lived as a child in a house full of books, there were shelves heavy with Victorian children's fiction by the likes of Mrs Molesworth. One such I liked but did not understand. The family lived in a castle in Alsace, and the eldest son is a cadet officer in the French Army. The girls' best-beloved cousin is the same, in the German Army. An early scene shows the two boys admiring one another's brand-new uniforms; the girls bursting with love and pride. This tale was full of heart-rending sentimental detail, including the Charge of the Cuirassiers at Reichshoffen. Both boys of course are killed. Before laughing (memory enriches one with these farcical Nabokovian discoveries) I remind myself that such family circumstances were a commonplace. The book was called *The Castle of the White Flag* and was written by Evelyn Everett Green, a popular author for teenage girls of a type of novel that would have been called a *Backfisch-roman* (similar to Mills & Boon for soppy shopgirls).

The German administration was often coarsely oppressive. Notorious is the cobbler in Saverne (Zabern) shot for laughing at a pompous Prussian Lieutenant. And when history repeated itself in our own day, and Alsace was overrun anew by Hitler's Reich, matters were far far worse. As we shall see. But one must try to be fair. During those nigh fifty years of 1870–1918 the people here were probably happier and certainly more prosperous than under French rule. The proof (I must give evidence for this opinion, still thought outrageous) is that when the two provinces returned to France the people demanded – and obtained – that much of the German social legislation be kept unchanged. And that this is to this day the case.

This land is my home, through many years. Here in

France I myself and our children have settled, rooted, seeded: no one has more right, nor more authority, to speak as I please of France. Thus; La République is a great power, often enough deserving admiration, and my love. More rarely my respect. The rule of law is far too often subservient to the Raison d'Etat, which too often is merely the convenience and the fair face of the administration. Itself – too often – deeply corrupt and lethargically incompetent. There is far too much legislation and a notorious disregard for most of it; understandably since regulations are written in a bumbling officialese. Black mark for the language of Voltaire, contriving to be both obscure and ambiguous. Naturally, I have nothing to say about English or German government. One will have to do one's best to see that the Community's already notorious bureaucracy in Brussels will learn lessons from the shortcomings of all three. Which is unlikely.

At this point the history of Grandfontaine is heavily overlaid by war. That, inevitably, must be given a separate section of narrative.

4

THE WARS

'**O**UR' WAR OF 1935–45 was after the initial stage of the 'phony war' largely a war of movement. In this, the line of the Vosges and the tactical positioning of Grandfontaine played little role. There was bitter fighting southward, around Saint Dié and the 'Colmar pocket'. Even the liberation of the village was not made without destruction, death. Taking a larger view, nothing much to speak of. One day there were Wehrmacht soldiers in Schirmeck and rumour of embittered defence of this famous (eminently defensible) line. The morn, there were unshaved chubby figures in American uniforms, grinning and handing out chewing-gum to pale meagre children. It all passed like a dream; suddenly we were all free. In the four years of the 1914–18 war it had been a very different matter.

Here, up the hill, a few minutes' walk from our house, in 1870, was established 'the border'. I must hope that I have made clear that this, the line of the Vosges summits, was and is indeed a 'frontier'.

It was not always very clearly delimited or marked. But in woodland clearings majestic Kaiserliche imperial customs officials – any German bureaucracy is quite as pompous and obscurantist as our own – scowled at their French counterparts. One must acknowledge that now and then a hot cup of coffee or a little glass of schnapps on a winter morning pushed a tight hat back upon a sweaty forehead. Belts were sometimes loosened. There'd have been a bit of smuggling – bit of bribery too no doubt. People with family on both sides. Notices saying ACHTUNG. In the village everyone knew where to cross if they had business on the other side. In 1940 they still knew, and the 'Passeurs', the guides to obscure paths, got many people out of the Reich, weren't always paid, sometimes left their own skin.

Meantime French troops crept up to the Vosges crests and fortified them. By 1914 they were throughly prepared, with supply lines and munition dumps. The German Army knew all about it, unfussed. From the summit of the Donon they could direct artillery with great accuracy. Today on the forest verges one finds the massive concrete housings of the big guns; there are casemates and bunkers.

The French would attack, firm believers in *la furia francese*. They did not know that here would be a foretaste of the blood-bath. One can't help wondering whether even now, close to ninety years after, France has managed to renew that lost blood. Everywhere the German armies held the better positions. And wasn't General Haig the guiltier, in stubborn arrogance and stupidity, when two years later he sent so many to die on the Somme? He must have known by then what to expect.

Here, lunatically, the French commander attacked the Donon, and won it. But behind lie other heights, and only ten miles on was waiting another agonizing defeat, and then they were back where they had started, here above Grandfontaine, and they would stay there another four years.

We called it the Great War in my childhood. Like so many more it was fought in this blood-fertilized heartland I call mine. The Englishman, familiar with what we vaguely call Flanders, scarcely realizes that the French-held line went on down to Switzerland. Aged twelve I had never heard of the Chemin des Dames. Or the height and hidden valleys of the Vosges. These are not simple pyramidal peaks. There are in fact two Donons with a saddle between. The second, 'le Petit', is the less majestic and perhaps the more terrible. In their assault upon the twin peak the French failed. The failure is marked in pitiful manner, movingly. The tombs are not the ranked and ordered white crosses familiar to us. They are the stones of the mountain.

In the ragged little band of German boys who clung on was a stonemason. He smoothed surfaces of rock with his chisel and carved what he knew simply, in the devout Gothic lettering of a Bavarian village cemetery. Some graves are named – his comrades. With the same care and respect he honours the boys he was told were his enemies. 'Here fell – three brave French soldiers!' Or five. Or nine. A company or regimental number. All the way up they lie. He must have been here for long; there are so many. Perhaps the tradition once established was carried on by others. One would like to think of some Colonel, man of civilized thought, writing a message back to Base – 'Send me a stone-cutter'. On the col called 'between the Donons' (there's a hikers' shelter there today, and the ashes of camp-fires) is the 'Schubertstein', anywhere else a conventional memorial; and at the summit quite a considerable surface carved and figured.

For after this battle, of a ferocity and futility astounding (but that we know Loos, and Neuve Chapelle, Beaumont Hamel, all those where a hundred thousand were lost for ten metres of mud won) the respective commanders stayed where they were. Both the German and French positions were too difficult to assault and impossible to turn. An immense quantity of shells were fired. Most of this is hidden now by the kindly forest.

A few stones today remain. Many have been vandalized, stolen, mutilated by brutal ignorant hands. Others overset or overgrown. If only one were left ninety years on it would speak louder than so many imbecile politicians. Some poet would say (I am paraphrasing from memory) 'God save the King, *Gott mit Uns*, God this, God that – *Mein Gott*, said God, I've got my work cut out'.

Since most unhappy of all there's more to come. 'Up the hill' the signs of 1914–18 are much blurred and often effaced, but 'down the hill' (clear to see from my garden) is another, more recent monument, just across the Bruche valley, above

Schirmeck. So that Grandfontaine sees and knows both. A needle of stone; it sparkles white in sunlight but not much sun shines there. For here is the Struthof, the extermination camp built by the Nazis; the only one on this side of the Rhine, and not on that account the least horrible.

I have to stop a second to take breath. Breathe deeply. If I were Jewish I would say the little prayer, the Kaddish.

At Schirmeck was the railhead. They built a transit camp here, those people, to hold deportees, the thousands destined for forced labour within the Reich. This is now obliterated, because far too many local people collaborated, betimes joyfully, with the regime, and in the years since an immense shame has been felt. Of the Schirmeck camp nothing can now be seen. But they felt the need – these people – for a more severe lesson to be taught to resistors. Eventually for the merely stroppy, guilty of insolence or derision. On the bleak hill above Natzwiller they built another prison camp, not just to hold but to exterminate.

I find it difficult to speak of this place, plainly, without sarcasms and without any literature. It is not one of the big machines capable of chewing up a thousand unpersons at a go. There are no spectacular works like the tunnel at Dora. Belongs, though, on the list.

It faces north; above the village a road serpentines up the hill, built by the prisoners, a stiffish climb to a plateau bitterly cold in winter and in summer a furnace. There is no way of ferrying in large convoys of chimney fodder. The Eichmann statisticians would have viewed it as awkward. But it accomplished all that was wished. The gas chamber is small; only a few at a time were called for showers.

But beyond the neat gateway (with the famous slogan arching above) the parade ground is spacious, and prominent at the head is the gallows, as though put there now to frighten tourists, a bit of Halloween humour. Down the slope the barrack emplacements are neatly, mathematically ranged. At the bottom two of the hutments stand intact; a little museum with the wooden frame for whipping people, and one of the cremation ovens.

Often I stand on the Donon pass, this antique gateway between France and Upper-Rhine. A tidy pattern unrolls, around. Above, the paths wind over the short grass into the massif, where the trees hide the slaughter. Beside me a hedge and a neat grassy plot, a few rows of little crosses betokening a 'real' military cemetery. Immediately beneath me the village nestles in its narrow glen, with the tiny spire of the church: simple and pretty. And across the valley the stone needle of the Struthof. In sunlight it twinkles at one.

There are those who will find me a bit sententious, about all this.

On the first of November – the Toussaint – people make pilgrimage to family graves; to clean and tidy them. Bringing flowers, and a night-light, in a little glass bowl against the draught. At eventide a brave sight. The top-heavy chrysanthemums, over-large and too brightly coloured, stand until overset by a gust of wind. One year when the children were small I took them up to the Struthof just to stand and look. It was real Toussaint weather; cold with a strong wind, now and then a shower of icy rain. The gallows stood there empty, rope and noose slowly twisting. I'm afraid I thought of Simon Tappertit. 'There is no resting place,' says Miss Miggs – sententiously – 'but in the silent tombs.' To which he rejoins – 'I wish you was in the silent tombs, I do, and locked up tight in a good strong'un.'

We have of course our own village cemetery, and our own little war memorial. I have my own candle, and my own personal chrysanthemum.

5

ANATOMY OF THE VILLAGE

A T THE FOOT OF THE DONON lies the little market town of Schirmeck which is our link with the outside world. Five kilometres down the winding mountain road; no distance in a car and everybody now has one. The stream called the Framont, assemblage of our four village brooks, swells the little river Bruche at Schirmeck, and this is our link with the Rhine. It follows the shortest route down the valley, but the old footpath alongside it is abandoned now and overgrown, and in winter choked with snow.

Schirmeck is abustle with traffic and heavy trucks wind up the Bruche valley and over the hills to Saint Dié sixty kilometres further; a passage to central and southern France. Through the foothills and across the Alsace plain to Strasbourg is a simpler run. The railway follows the same route, a country line now little used.

Strasbourg is modern Europe and you could get a plane to nigh anywhere. The Paris *autoroute* runs on through to Germany or south to Switzerland. Or a train – in the old days this was the first stop for the Orient Express on the romantic road to Istanbul. To reach Grandfontaine – even our house at the top end of this straggling village – is no great matter. The roads are all widened and resurfaced.

Thirty-five years ago it was a more primitive business: the car tacked from village to village with many awkward corners. It was thought of as a 'main road' and was kept swept. Only here was the snow packed and trodden hard; often one could barely climb our hill. In the historical perspective which here and to my eye is present and immediate, Grandfontaine was in winter almost isolated and had to learn a sturdy self-sufficiency. Like any other – English or Welsh – hill village.

Here comes an illustration, of quite a graphic sort.

In the very last house lives an old woman: she married into this house and has never left it. 'I was born in Malplaquet, my father held the hill farm. And my mother had a difficult labour; some complication, see? So he had to go for the doctor, to Schirmeck, walking down the river path, the snow to mid-thigh, see? That wasn't this doctor. His father, you know, le Père Schmitt. Who got out the horse and trap, the sleigh, more like. It wasn't too bad on the road as far as the Jeanne d'Arc but thereafter – no way. So he left the horse with the people of the pub and the last good three miles on his skis. Couple hours later he had me in his hands. And now here I am. There's more hereabout owe their lives to le Père Schmitt.' A banal story; any Yorkshire dale would tell the same. Easily verified; a half-dozen times we had to leave the car at the Jeanne d'Arc and walk uphill. One day in the doctor's consulting room I asked about the buildings at the back. 'Those are the stables,' smiling a little. 'Basic, in my grandfather's day.' Nowadays he has a Land Rover outside the door; four-wheel drive. The outlying district could still be hard sledding. One could easily imagine his father, robust old gentleman, swinging the starting handle on a big 1920s Renault; but just a little further back...

On the corner of the road (it will wind in hairpins a further five kilometres up to the Donon pass) the Jeanne d'Arc stands today, massive (above the pub are a dozen hotel rooms) by the bridge over the Framont: it is the entry point of Grandfontaine. The narrow brook-dug valley is in fact four narrow sharp-cut glens. The anatomy is that of your outspread left hand, palm foremost. Only the little finger is missing, and that is a frequent accident here: the woodcutters have often lost more. The water of the brooks is the blood of the hand, gathered at the base into the Framont, a pulsing and turbulent artery.

At this nexus stood the Framont forges which worked the iron of the mines, and of these I will have much to say. The village tells now three hundred souls but in the nineteenth century over a thousand. There were six pubs, my own house among them, but even The Jeanne d'Arc, busy and convivial when we came, is still and shuttered now. The nerve-centre is in the palm, where the school – thank heaven – is still alive, and Thérèse, the village shop, and the Mairie shows a more pompous front than when it was the presbytery. To care for Administration instead of souls is a falling-off, I should think, but the Mayor's self-importance is greatly swollen.

Look still at the outspread hand. The thumb at the bottom going off at a sharp angle is important; named 'Le Haut Fourneau' after the forge buildings. A peaceful valley now that the workshops are gone, stretching away to the hamlet of Salm and the ruined castle at the summit ... but now we have to climb to the top of the palm and the three stretched fingers. Of these the forefinger is the route des Minières, by far the most important since without the mines Grandfontaine would have no reason for existing at all. At the top of these bored and tunnelled hillsides wells up the source of the *grand fontaine* itself; strong and never-failing spring, now channelled underground, down the hill to Schirmeck.

The other two fingers are important to the people living there: a valley abrupt and stony, for it leads straight into the Donon massif, called the 'Goutte Ferry' ('goutte' is a Vosges word for a mountain brook as well as for the little cheering glass of schnapps); the last finger runs to rejoin the Donon road at the hairpin called the Mossy Bridge; this valley is flatter than the others and is named, a bit condescendingly, 'La Basse'. But a pretty stream, widening into sandy pools, with tiny trout, heron-haunted.

At the top of the palm – for this metaphor must replace a sketch map where the lines cross and run downwards towards the wrist – the three brooks join, and have been dammed into a pretty, tree-lined village pond. The overflow is the Framont. At the bottom of the village, where the Haut Fourneau brook comes in, the whole complex gave the power needed for the wheels, stamps, hammers of the forge. Even in the dry season, the droughty August, these hill-fed, rain-watered hydraulics have formidable strength.

Everywhere the water has been constrained by the massive masoned blocks lifted from Roman and perhaps Celtic works. In the channels are rusty little lock-gates, weirs and canals and rams. One can still trace the skills, often highly sophisticated, where water gave power. The power that even on the humblest scale mankind searches for and takes advantage from.

The unusual abundance and year-long reliability of this power, together with the mineral resources, gave the village an industrial nature. In so humble and primitive a context the word sounds odd. To my generation 'industry' meant the massive piles of smoke-blackened brick, the Black Country, the mill towns of the North and the Ruhr. Even today the word 'power' summons pictures of the cooling towers of atomic energy, the monstrous pylons supporting high tension-lines. A younger generation will see harmless-looking sheds of plastic and aluminium, clean and silent, almost unobtrusive, where they make the electronic bits and pieces for the modern version of power. Nobody looking at Grandfontaine today would find any hint of either word. Most people indeed still see the whole of France as primordially an agricultural country.

The Vosges villages were indeed rural in the highland, Welsh or Scottish sense; a few fields of corn in the sunnier valleys, upland pasturage for a few sheep and a cow or two; all very small and a bit pathetic.

One sees then, often, surprisingly, largish buildings of an undoubtedly industrial nature, nothing dark or satanic but indubitably mills. To the immediate question comes a simple answer: there were a hundred and more little textile factories. Labour was cheap and so was water-power. The name

'Boussac', famous in my lifetime, had here a particular reso-
nance. Cotton thread came down from the spinning centres
of Roubaix and Tourcoing, was here woven into sheets and
pillowcases; was finished into *bonneterie*: each little workshop
had its speciality; shirts or handkerchiefs, bras or knickers:
in Schirmeck 'La Rubanerie' made straps no doubt and sus-
penders – and the Boussac empire wove it all into a coherent
whole. In Grandfontaine there were two of these little textile
mills.

One has only to look at a contour map. Even the central
'palm' dale is too narrow for more than the tiniest of cultivated fields, while the others are mere clefts in the rock.
Look for comparison at hill villages where the houses are in
chalet style, lifted on wooden supports and the beasts housed
beneath. A house here is itself of mineral character, of stone
throughout with the foundation excavated deeply: burrows.
This house can be tall, of unexpectedly generous and airy
proportion, but has a noticeable goblin style. The Vosges
fermette (mine is a good example) was a farm in a sense almost toylike: the working area had space for two cows, two
horses, and a cart – like a model made for children to play
with – with a little flagged room behind for a very small
family of piggies, and a barn above just the right size for the
hay off our meadow. This was juxtaposed to the living area
and is now an integral part of it. In front was a little kitchen
garden, and space enough to range a few chickens. Once the
family subsistence was met there would have been very little
surplus produce.

The two little textile mills were not of great importance in
the life of the village. One still stands, a gaunt barrack which
nobody would take the trouble to knock down. The stream
was dammed to fill a reservoir, and turbines gave the power
to drive machinery. They brought some prosperity; perhaps
fifty village women worked here and earned a contribution to
domestic finance, and that would be precious. In this essentially male world of hard physical work it is difficult to see

exactly how great the role they played in local economics. A
manager no doubt and a technician overseer, both from 'outside'; a clerical bod for accountancy. The village contributed
perhaps a timekeeper, an engine-room mechanic, and 'the
girls', some half-dozen of whom might have been charge
hands with more skills and some responsibility. It might
have been semi-finished work of little sophistication, because
down the hill were many other larger and more elaborate
factories of greater importance. They closed only a year or
two before we came here, no longer economically viable, and
I have never heard anything to suggest that the loss was
deeply felt. Still, there they are or were, for the second and
larger was on the crossroads where the 'fingers join the
palm' and is now demolished – to make room for a half-
dozen new houses. I am sorry, for they were part of our
historical fabric.

The village has changed much within the last few years.
This has been, mostly, of social significance. A local reflection of the ways in which all of Europe has changed ... that,
in turn, is not my purpose. Some of the changes have been
anatomical and these here give me pause. When, though, we
came here, the physical aspect of Grandfontaine had altered
very little over a hundred years, so that I am a good witness
to this. The house that we bought, indeed, seems to me
pivotal to the life the village led. So that here is where I wish
to start upon the sociology.

6

SOCIOLOGY OF THE VILLAGE

O R – how humourless can one get? I was reminded, as I often am, of Kipling's ferocious farce, 'The Village that voted the Earth was Flat.' The master embellished, as his habit was: after cutting a narration to the limits of a reader's understanding (even it is sometimes thought beyond, though this is not one of his obscurer tales) he liked to put in what he called illuminations and arabesques. In this story there are many; one of the better ones is 'a scholarly middle in the *Spectator* entitled "Village Hausmania"'. When, after finding myself direly pompous, I am tempted to take refuge in irony, I must remind myself – remind a reader – that it would be out of key and out of drawing; catch hold of any metaphor you like. 'Village Hausmania' has indeed overtaken Grandfontaine, but only within the last few years, in the person of the Mayor. Monsieur le Maire is certainly a subject for farce, in France always has been, but is out of place in these lines.

Again, for the point has been made before, I try to look with the eyes I had thirty-five years ago, when the village had changed little over twice that number. One did lay eyes on the mayor from time to time, chalky old gentleman with silver bristles. He liked things left as they were; not only a French habit.

The house was a village landmark. A *fermette* like so many. Some description has been made, and more detail will be given, but in brief it was and is the last house of the village proper, a staging post on the climb to the Minières, some seven hundred metres up the hill. In the past it had been a bakery – of which some trace survives – and very recently it had been an *estaminet* or drinking shop, called Au Moulin.

As Village ancients who remember drinking here tell me, but memory – the mill, if mill there was, must have been across the road, where the stream runs. Upon a time they ground corn there, and here opposite they baked bread with the flour ... But the grog-shop, for so one must describe it – that is vivid because I have seen it; starting point, I have said, pivotal, to this book. Not a pub, or café. There wasn't even beer, I should think, because there is no room for it. A cup of coffee, maybe. A glass of wine, probably. But essentially *la goutte*, the Alsace-Lorraine schnapps, the white fruit-alcohol in the long bottle, familiar in restaurants today.

A panelled room, with two windows overlooking the roadway and a third facing downhill; one could see what was going on. Three long oblong tables (at one of these I am writing) and wooden benches. In the corner a little counter, behind the stove, with zinc shelves – a cupboard in the thickness of the wall, for bottles. In that corner a grandfather clock, likewise set back into the wall, ticked; it still does, ringing and repeating the hours in a thin silvery chime.

Why just at this point? Why was it important? That is quite easily reconstructed and understood.

Above the village, in the Minières, the iron ore was loaded on to little tipper-trucks (one or two still exist). These trundled downhill by gravity upon a miniature rail line – and lengths of this too can still be seen outside houses, to keep stacked firewood from the wet ground. The ore travelled thus to the forges at the bottom of the village, over a mile, and some braking system must at moments have been needed. The empty trucks had to be towed back by horse or mule. This minuscule and primitive system served certainly for some hundreds of years: the ore was rich, of high quality. Many men were busied with this transport. The reason for the drinking shop becomes clear. The horses were breathed half-way up the hill (their drinking troughs are still there). The men took a breath in harmony. The owner here would have had a niceish little business, seeing and knowing everything that went on. Smart too, no doubt. Drinks went on the slate; Johnny – three goes of schnapps. If he couldn't pay a deal might be struck; little corner of land perhaps changed hands.

Harsh work, vile in the mines. But a pattern begins to emerge of a people poor but not pinched; a hardy folk and healthy, narrow but independent of mind. Wood was plentiful and the houses well heated. Bacon hung to cure in these broad chimneys. The smallest cabin had a patch for vegetables, a few chickens and a cage for rabbits; a fruit tree or two; potatoes in the cellar and apples in the attic. Bread of barley and rye and none the worse for that. Often a sheep and a goat to nibble the woodland fringe, keep back the sempiternal bramble. Some had bees. The streams were diverted into many pools where trout could be raised. The meadows were full of wild strawberries and in the woods mushrooms were plentiful (the treasured *cèpe*). The Princes of Salm exacted no doubt high taxes, and the Republic when it came ground finer and harder; a crowd of bureaucratic exactions. As far as one can judge there was little misery and apart from rheumatism little illness. But there was a great deal of hardship, and a good deal of death.

The Minières, a kilometre up the road, is a *cuvette*, a shallow saucer of grassland in the woods surrounding, full of snow in winter but in the summertime open and sunny. Nowadays a hamlet of thirty-odd houses, many used only in holiday time. There are traces of many more, little cabins long demolished. At the head, it is thought there was once a church. In the centre is a biggish house with a bell turret on the roof: almost within living memory this was the school. No doubt of it, a century ago some hundred or two people lived here – and more came daily, to work.

At the foot, beside the roadway, are three archways, masonry of dressed stone. One is only a drainage outlet but on it is carved the crossed hammers, symbol of the mine and its workings. One entrance has been restored, and visitors may view some hundred metres of shaft and gallery. A hut has been built to house a little museum with samples of the many interesting minerals found here, and there is a variety of goblin tools and appliances. This is goblin country: in the woods around, if you know where to look for them, are caverns and holes, for there were many other mines. At this, the principal seam of high-quality ore, one can see the beginnings of a shaft long drowned in water and the emplacement of pumping mechanisms. The never-ending problem was to work bent double and knee- or even waist-deep in the ever-seeping water.

We may guess that Romans, perhaps even Celts, knew of this ore. The earliest written mention is in 1260; it was to remain famous for six centuries. The iron holds traces of tungsten and nickel, giving a natural tensile toughness. So that here in Grandfontaine were forged unusually good tools and weapons.

Twice in my memory prospectors have come to drill for samples. Was there perhaps uranium? One is glad to say that the percentages of desirable goodies were found too low to be worth the trouble of exploiting today.

The discovery of the big Lorraine ironfields, the proximity of coal and railways, the invention of the steel process – all this should have put paid to these wretched little diggings by say 1850. The reputation of the forges, the metallurgical skills, prolonged the life of these mines. In 1870 it is said that they were turning out the barrels and lock mechanisms of the Chassepot rifle, but this, the story of the forges, must be described separately. The mines are important since through them runs the life-blood of the village, which without them would not exist. As with the *grand fontaine* itself, it is enough that they are there. The interest cannot compare, objectively, with the larger and better-preserved works at Sainte Marie, thirty kilometres to the south.

Still, there came a time when the iron of the Framont mines was famous, and was of weight in the counsels of Europe. In a village nearly anywhere a tourist can often find reason to pause for an hour. There might be a little guide-book due to local pieties and enthusiasms. A historic house or beautiful garden, at a pinch the site of a battlefield. Perhaps even by some miracle an unspoiled corner, haunt of rare bird or butterfly. Such reasons have in Grandfontaine been effaced by the carelessness, malice, or greed of men. This also is why I have tried to search out and restore, endeavour to put in writing – since this skill I possess – something of this long and rich history.

7

THE FRAMONT FORGES

A T THE FOOT OF THE VILLAGE, just where the roadway
I called the thumb branches away from the palm, and
the brooks join together at the wrist to tumble on down to
Schirmeck, stands a simple unpretentious eighteenth-century
manor-house. Of some size and fine proportions but now
dilapidated and neglected-looking, shadowed by overgrown
laurel and rhododendron: nothing is left of the once-fine
gardens and orangery. At the side rusty gates of good iron-
work open to a grass-grown courtyard, and beyond are
stables, estate office and a little clock-tower. Plainly it was
once a house of importance. On both sides the streams have
been bridged with the plain, fine stonework of an earlier age
and all around can be glimpsed massive ruins, but so
tumbled (as though by bombardment) and ivy-grown that no
purpose can now be distinguished. This was the house of
Louis Champy, the Ironmaster, and the ruins are all that
remain of the eighteenth- century forges. Only the name
given the roadway survives – *Le Haut Fourneau*.

There was no single vast building. In those days an iron-
works was housed in a chain of smaller workshops for each
separate process; the crushers, stamps and hammers; the
low and the high furnaces. If only they had kept this wonderful complex intact – there would have been something for
the guidebook!

My guess (it can be no more) is that the people, the villagers, hated it: that it was a symbol of serfdom and oppression;
that as soon as they could – no tales are told – they destroyed
it. We will see that another similar symbol was here also
effaced, and there is no sign of where it stood.

Of these buildings one survived to our time. It stood there

isolated at the meeting of roads, a shapely piece of stone-work, house-sized yet not a house so that its purpose was difficult to guess. It was the Maréchalerie, a blacksmith's shop, where the many horses were shod and handtools were fashioned, and we may guess the smaller spare parts of machinery. Only a few years ago it burned down and a bulldozer cleared the blackened masonry. A strange accident! I enquired; the mayor told me blandly that 'the road needed widening anyhow'. Quite: standing in the way of progress. This handsome and historic building might have housed a notable museum. But that is not the way village politics function.

One piece of fortune, if very small, was left to us. In the archives at Epinal survived a ground plan of the whole. House and gardens, orangery, even the barracks built to house workers. And the different forge buildings, Basse and Haut Fourneau, la Renardière where the ore was purified ... and there are some fuzzy, poor-quality engravings of oddly-shaped goblin structures. Le Martinet – the big hammer.

Below the bridge, where the footpath will open and follow the course of the stream down to Schirmeck, is a jungle of overgrown vegetation. A few steps further is a lake, dark from the trees pressing upon it, sinister and heron-haunted. This is the reservoir built in 1760 by Pierre Launay to power the forges, of shapely stones taken (I should think probably) from the much older buildings on the Donon. Here the overflow fall still trickles down; young trees have forced their way through joints. The juicy green of summer feels close to tropical: one could believe oneself in Angkor.

Further down still, beyond these ruins, stands a Piranesi, still largely intact; the last remnant of all, added to the complex in the mid-nineteenth century – the rolling-mill. Megalomania, for by then the forges were at their last gasp, but magnificent, from the stream side an arched vista full of ghosts. From the road can be seen the high chimney: a tree grows in derision at its summit.

The valley widens below. Here the owner built himself a palace in the worst of neo-Renaissance taste, fit for an industrial magnate. It stood for barely thirty years. Not a stone remains upon another. But for a pillared gateway it might never have been. Who tore it down? The villagers? – this is an enigma. Nobody speaks of it. There are legends of orgies – seduced housemaids – meals served by naked girls – all such houses have these tales.

I will prefer to walk back up the phantom path to the old house remaining. Louis Champy lived here, ironmaster through the glory years; a remarkable man. Imagination would not serve; this history is in the archives of the Préfecture of the Vosges at Epinal.

Before the Revolution, in royalist times, this source of wealth was in dispute. The Princedom of Salm, the Duchy of Lorraine; one is yet again in a frontier land; the rich Abbey of Senones would also have fingers in this pie. Champy began as man-of-affairs and agent for the princely owner. But at the Revolution these feudal enclaves were swept away and their Lords retired to estates in Germany. The Préfecture, then as now rigid, narrow, fussy, made Champy's life a misery. Bombarding him with paperwork. The returns were inexact or incomplete; there wasn't enough money coming in; they were quite sure he had too many employees, and how many of these were foreigners, draft-dodgers, undesirables of every sort? Then, as now. In his hey-day Champy had over a thousand people working for him here in Grandfontaine.

He understood bureaucracies. He'd sent in all the papers. Confused and mislaid no doubt by incompetent prefectorial clerkdom. Then, as now. He strengthened his position until able to offer the Republic a large lump sum in return for undisputed ownership: they snapped it up.

Affairs were prosperous. Contracts for cannons from the Swiss and even the Dutch. The high quality of this iron has been remarked. While Napoleonic wars raged, one need have no doubt that Champy, like every arms dealer before and since, sold to both sides. What were the realities?

Ore, extracted here, in the Minières, in the cramped water-logged galleries. It trundled down the hill; we saw my house a half-way stage for men and horses. To power machinery Champy had the never failing water, ingeniously controlled by the locks and dams which stretched far back into the hills. Much still visible . . .

He needed fire. No coal was available. Wood alone could not give him temperatures high enough. His foresters ranged afield, built the secret fires for the Black Art which would distill – as it were drop by drop – the charcoal over days and nights of cunning skill. Certainly he was as good an engineer as he was administrator. The archives speak of experts come to advise upon the mine-workings (never satisfactory) and to admire the techniques of his iron foundry. It is arresting to think of this settlement, so obscure in the labyrinth of hills, rivalling the most famous of armourers.

Hard-head. A brute? A driver. He built barracks for his workers and how did he feed them? He wrote furiously to the Prefect: 'If you want iron, send me corn.' We can hear of him, in his town house – the rue des Juifs in Strasbourg – bargaining with the Commissaires who supplied the armies; Count Daru perhaps (Stendhal's chief). An honest man? According to his lights, no doubt; he was dealing with people who understood weapons. Like General Rapp, the gunner from Colmar; another hard-head, who when Napoleon enquired the marching distance between Madrid and Warsaw grunted out 'Too far' – but the Emperor didn't listen.

An Irishman in the woods of Parnell's Wicklow estate said, 'I see him out here sometimes, but sure it's only an illusion'. Just so I like to think I can catch a glimpse of Le Père Champy, in the high-collared coat and twice-wound stock of his portrait engraved in those Empire years, stumping bullish round his domain. For years he was Mayor, Grandfontaine his heart and blood. A thick silver-mounted cane, high polished boots, gold watch-chain across a bright blue waistcoat. Who would have a better right to haunt the village? A square obstinate face full of character, alert piggy eyes, heavy chin. I see him badly shaved because always in a hurry. That path, down from his house along the jungly waterside, became a haunt of my own. One never meets anyone else there.

8

Village Psychologies

O UT WALKING, I come daily upon them. They will be puttering around their doorstep; the classic chore of 'fetching in wood'. (A Bretonne granny when asked by her daughter what on earth she was doing replied invariably 'Putting the parsley to keep fresh'.) This eddying movement stops. *'Bonjour. On se promene?'* This greeting is invariable. 'No; spying' would not be thought in the least funny, though they relish a joke. We will exchange pleasantries about rheumatism and the state of the nation, and go on our way refreshed. Throughout, the eye roves: not a flicker anywhere escapes it. Only Eugène stands stock still, the gaze fixed upon a distant star: when I speak he will give a great start.

This holds good for no more than half the populace. Elsewhere the brow clouds, the eye slews sidelong, the bonjour is as tight and suspicious as it has been these thirty years. A spy undoubted. *L'étranger*, the foreigner. English, which is worst of all.

The French house is a fortress; that is cliché. The neighbour on a Paris landing might after twenty years let fall a 'Looks like rain' (amid a clash of many keys and bolts) but here in the country silence. Never will you see the inside of a house. This state of affairs is perfectly well known: none of that damned American neighbourliness. In the Latin south, in the warm, Belgian north, the poorer the house the bigger the welcome. Not in France . . .

Here it is easier to understand. A mountain village – even those from the next hamlet are foreigners here. A mountain people whose life has never been easy. And upon a frontier; small wonder that the mentality prevails of 'we only want to be left alone'. But to say, condescendingly, that they're a backward lot, is superficial.

They are a healthy and vigorous race. Inbred, incestuous they doubtless are: one would expect dwarfs, goitrous mental-deficients. It is not the case. The lumpen, those whose dough has never risen, these we have as everywhere from Labrador to Guadeloupe: they are of no race nor country. Few here are deformed or defective, and fewer wrecks, abandoned to their suffering. The children are sturdy and bright of eye. The family – that traditional French nucleus now alarmingly looser and becoming disrupted – is here still intact. Tight, jealously possessive. Can one wonder at the slogans of 'Parents, I hate you' now so widespread? But it could well be thought here that the intense, antique social cement has a virtue outweighing the obvious countercharges. A proudly independent people here still. Granny has become an alarming, even dangerous old pest? It is plainly time for Grandpa to be put down? Their dignity will be kept intact. Common form across the world is that the launching of children upon the world is ever more lengthy, difficult and expensive. Here, still, no sacrifice will be thought too much. The children do not forget. Here, every weekend, you see the cars arrive; the young family with wife and baby, bringing a cake. Granny, happy, putting the water on for coffee. The antique nineteenth-century pattern persists. Of a Sunday evening you will see the cars nose to tail streaming back to the towns. Here they are washing-up, aglow with joy and pride. I do not think the sentimental view in the least misplaced. Love and security mean more to a child than anything, and if that sounds like *Froggy's Little Brother* then I'll come out in defence of Victorian sentimental novels. The village can also be a place of ruffianly coarseness, offensive to my citified sensibilities.

How much has it changed, in these thirty-five years – an entire generation – of our living here, and to me that seems so short a time; can I illustrate? Outwardly, a good deal, perhaps a great deal, as has the whole of rural France. But inwardly? Perhaps through anecdote?

With the closing of the mines and the forges, in the closing years of the last century, Grandfontaine reverted to the village's earliest vocation, which was woodcutting. I will have to treat this at some length; for now I need only remark that it is a harsh life. The woodsman was paid for quantity, for long hours beginning and ending in darkness, for floundering in snow and ice, for haste. No family but had lost a man under falling trees. There is nothing exceptional about this: any Breton or Norman fishing village has the same story to tell. By our time the terrible axes had been replaced broadly by the chain-saw, but safety was a luxury no one could afford. Firewater was the panacea. With plenty of schnapps fisherman or woodsman deadened the pain and forgot the risk. A mutilated hand or foot was a signmanual in these trades.

A son of mine tells this story. It is not long ago; he might have been seventeen at the time. The children were at school in Strasbourg but we spent our weekends here.

'I hitched a lift, coming down off the Donon. Broken old truck, back from the forest going home, totally pissed, naturally. Driver stopped for me, shouts "Oh Joseph – get up". Skeleton sat up at the back, two fingers on one hand and one on the other. Said "Oh, what a beautiful boy". Thought rape was going to be the least of my troubles. A hundred an hour, downhill on the curves. Passed a broken tree he said "Was that where we crashed last week?" My life or my arse, which was it to be?' Nothing really out of the way here, except that 'Joseph, get up' passed instantly into family folklore.

The next comes from a neighbour; a serious, indeed sober man. 'I was in the forest; met these two loonies; they had a loaded trailer, ran out on the curve and tipped, on the soft edge. Nothing unusual about that; I went to lend them a hand. Saw then the third; he's under the trailer, pinned by the leg. They can't straighten up and they can't get him out, these two jackasses, so they're arguing. "Give him a good dose of schnapps, we'll take his leg off with the saw." I yelled at them. "Drunken cunts, unload the trailer." They'd never thought of that; hadn't even entered their minds.'

The village has got a lot quieter. To be sure, it's only ten years since one notorious oldie managed to tip into the brook on his way home from the pub and drown in shallow water ... In the north, cirrhosis of the liver is still a major cause of death: the drunks of rural France still are the biggest source of road accidents in Europe. Times don't change that fast.

The courtship rituals haven't changed much either. The tiny girls seen playing on doorsteps were suddenly pushing prams of their own: the test of nubility, crude and vigorous, pastis in the pub and whipping her smartish into the bushes, is I should think unimpeded by contraceptive advertisements.

The last anecdote is my own and will be told at length, for it concerns a crime. This did not happen here but in a Vosges valley of the same nature, not at all far away. Here also we have crimes; they are not spoken of; officially they are not known. That old man alluded to, who fell late one night into a few inches' depth of the brook ... but certainly he was very drunk. Kipling wrote a remarkable story about the stream at the bottom of his garden. Told by one old man to another in a field. They speak softly, and they leave a good deal out. The story is called 'Friendly Brook' and there is precious little difference between our Framont and the Dudwell in Kipling's Sussex a hundred years before.

This crime became a *cause célèbre* and all of Europe rang with it. The difference is that this was not a dirty and drunken old pest but a little boy of two. A wise policeman knows when not to look, because looking will do no one any good. Here, the gendarmerie were forced to an enquiry, and a young magistrate forced by his own inexperience to believe in a deliberate and a dreadful crime. The friendly brook has great energy in flood time, and may in local belief have occult powers. This child was found hands tied with string but showing no other sign of violence. The fact which set the world aflame was that a little boy had apparently been killed by someone known and trusted, perhaps loved. Perhaps, horrible thought, his own mother.

The French judicial system is admirable when free of political pressure. Penal procedure is thoughtful, equitable, serene. It has the disadvantage, like many French institutions, of being complex and elaborate. Ruin, here, overtook it. Why was the preliminary enquiry negligent, incompetent, suspected of collusion? (Even in rural districts the gendarmerie are able and experienced professionals.) Why was vital forensic evidence lost, misplaced or tampered with? (The presence of water in the child's lungs was not clearly established.) A young, opinionated judge of instruction failed to control the technical research, leaked tendentious details to journalists, formed convictions and refused to alter them. In short, a dreadful botch.

Two appalling events complicated the disaster. The village, and in particular the family, was victimized by a poison pen of the worst sort; violent, obscene, illiterate, hideously gloating. Nastiest of all, showing a close knowledge of family thought and behaviour. The child's father, fairly out of his mind, formed the conviction that the murderer was his brother-in-law and neighbour; marched across with a shotgun; killed the man on his doorstep.

The press got into a frenzy. We know this story well. Their claim is that we enjoy few freedoms, and that their own freedom to comment must not be infringed. Comment in France will be pushed beyond the limits of fairness even in a case *sub judice*. This is the fault of governments ever since the Republic was founded. They have always attempted to control, censor and stifle opinion while paying a greasy lip-service to the liberty of expression . . .

At this pass an appalled and exasperated Public Prosecutor took an extreme step, if technically within his legal powers. He annulled the entire enquiry, discharged (the original meaning of this word is 'I relieve you of responsibility') the instructing judge, named a respected former President of the

Appeal Court to head an entire new search into the whole affair *ab initio*. This would be conducted – upon an inescapably blurred and trampled terrain – by the Police Judiciaire at Nancy. The gendarmerie swallowed this extreme insult in silence, perhaps thankful. The second enquiry reached a conclusion: by now inescapable; that the young mother must be brought to justice and to trial. Grave and heavy evidence (so much else was by now tautology) lay against her. The worst, an alleged writing and posting of the poison-pen letters. The last, and the most horrible, read 'Now I have my revenge. I'm loving it'.

Tried she was, on the capital charge, before the jury of ordinary men and women, and she was acquitted, for the lack of conclusive proof. And she was awarded a large sum in damages against the newspapers. I think most of that went to pay lawyers. Perhaps it did her some good. In Sartre's phrase 'hell is other people'. Some of it anyhow. She'd be well placed to give an opinion.

Because it still wasn't finished. During all this time her husband was sitting in jail, waiting to be tried himself for assassinating his brother-in-law – that essential and now silenced witness who might have been something more.

I could have written about all this. I could have been offered a lot of money for doing so; been given a press card and sat in court with the others who are there to describe dramatic moments. Instinct led me to refuse. There is also a good reason why fiction writers should not attempt this sort of work: they begin to see real human beings as figments of their own imagination. A nefarious instance of professional deformation. Now that the people concerned have moved out of that glaring light and, one must hope are at peace, now I can say something. There is a better light, and it shines on the village, and in this one can also see the comic.

Of the man's formal guilt there was of course no doubt. A crime of passion. In a French court the suffering is admitted. There is a traditionally moderate requisition from the prosecutor – at times generous – and a traditionally humane sentence.

It was though hoped that this might be at last the occasion for bringing the whole horribly knotted story out into daylight. To the credit of the Republic must go its very best effort; the full majesty of the Assize Court in Dijon. The presiding judge, eminent jurist, was known also as an exceptionally humane and patient man. After minute preparation there would be the most searching examination and cross-questioning by the best of legal talent. The President would make the most solemn charge to 'the village'. Now at last, emotion stilled, was the moment to speak out without fear: we must know, now, the truth.

The truth: the very last thing the village wanted ... Our affair into which no Court, no State, and no Press is going to poke its nose.

The young couple, dulled by utter exhaustion, repeated the whatever, said and resaid over four years. That had been expected. But there had been hopes of the village: of the postman, of the old woman pasturing her cows by the roadside, the old man who had been out with his dog. Above all, of a young girl, who said she knew; that she had seen; she had said so. To be sure she had also said the exact opposite. To the gendarmes, to the Police Judiciaire, to the journalists. Now to the three judges, gentle and quiet voiced (the one in the middle can be terrifying). The red robed Attorney-General soft-spoken but razor edged. The multitude of black gowns falsely sympathetic, the syrupy sidelong and implacable tormentors. She was round of face and square of body, stubbornly red-haired, exceedingly plain. Backward, to be sure, but no doctor could be found to call her deficient in understanding. She had been sixteen then, was now twenty. The poor dim little thing could set at defiance the sharpest minds of the Republic. If one could set aside the tragedy, the little boy in the cemetery, the grave covered with flowers, then it was risible. Farcical.

They could not understand, these lawyers, that their justice has no place in the algebra of clan relations. The equations, to them clear-cut, had to her no beginning nor end. I don't know. I can't remember. I said things put in my mouth. I was frightened.'

Instinctively this child knew every trick of the witness box. Melting into tears, losing her voice, asking for glasses of water, appealing faintly for protection. Faced with the crudest contradictions never outfaced. 'How do you explain that?' 'I don't explain it at all.' *'Je ne me l'explique pas'* is atavistic village bedrock. In a way, I feel proud of her.

And the young man? – for he was little past boyhood. A mild sentence; he had had four horrible years in prison. That far, justice functioned. I can, also, feel sympathy with the local gendarmes. Those inspectors and technicians of the Police Judiciare could never have understood a thing; they were townspeople.

The killing of a child, innocence assassinated, wrenched this village out of a subterranean organic life. The alimentary canal, its eating and sleeping habits, digestive processes and sexual fantasies, brought under a merciless light. For a modern police force works like that. 'Function normally, do you? Since every time there was something to see or to hear, you're there on the pot.' The poison pen letters got the same treatment. 'Take this piece of paper. Write to my dictation. You do know, do you, how to read and write?'. The village would feel an intense, an implacable hostility. Make head or tail, will you? What head, and what tail? As well ask questions of the friendly brook.

Sociology is mostly rubbish anyhow, resting as it does upon masses of bogus statistics: which of you ate cornflakes this morning? Or the 'day's work' in the gendarmerie. 'Quiet on the whole. A few auto accidents. There was the woman stark naked on the roof of a car.'[4] 'Oh yes and there were the nine garden dwarfs found hanging from a bridge, with a

4. I was reminded of Dickens' Bob Sawyer, whose progress while drunk by stage-coach is a famous set-piece.

notice saying we are a persecuted sect and have decided upon collective suicide.' A footnote to this report read 'No such objects have been reported stolen in this sector'. There is not a great deal of room for humour.

Village criminology: here in Grandfontaine we have our frauds and thieveries; the petty malignancies. The worst to happen to me was petrol poured on young flowering plants. One knows who and one knows why; there's nothing one can do about it. There will be – no doubt at all – more deep-seated evil. Like most serious crime this does not appear in statistics. Any village doctor signs a good few death certificates he knows very well to be bogus. The pillow on Granny's head? The man who fell off the step-ladder. That child who hadn't learned clean habits. We prefer not to know.

Don't lets think about death: think of life. Think for example of a Sunday. As an experiment, cross the Donon on a Sunday morning. You are in 'France' and there is already a Latin flavour in the air. The baker is open, smelling of fresh bread and of the traditional cake, to pick up on the way back from Mass. The butcher is open, and the flower shop. But here, even on the frontier, this is Alsace. The men overshaved, stiff in the good suit, the women bonneted and tripping daintily in high heels. Catching sight of the mill chimney I could picture myself in a nineteenth-century print; perhaps a wooded valley in Connecticut; paternalist owners laying down strict rules for the godly behaviour of the mill girls, to the high approval of Mr Dickens (freshly disembarked). It is another illusion: they are all over fifty and the younger generation is abed. The reflection is less of deeply-held German Christianity than of the intense conservatism of rural France. Undoubtedly, Louis Champy saw to it (with a woe-betide) that his flock went to Mass on Sunday and gave thanks ...

French, likewise deeply, are our local politics. The country-side votes for local notables; careful paternalist men (no women) with an intricate local network. A Deputy to the national Parliament (the Palais-Bourbon, well-named, in Paris) will be a mayor, a regional councillor deeply embedded, distributor of little local favours, a master of the windy rhetoric familiar also to English listeners. Over the last hundred years there has been precious little change in this pattern ... it would be very rare hereabout to find a Socialist. The Vosges region is a stronghold of the Church, of bigotry hand in glove with finance. Here you find a prudent, protectionist and reactionary nationalism; a deep distrust of anything new. This one could say to be held in common with all of rural France. It is all there, bitter and funny, in the pages of Stendhal. The marriage alliance to a Notable, the importance of a friendly ear in Paris, the embezzlement of the orphanage's funds and finding cosy jobs for incompetent relations; now, as ever. Here, as anywhere, they are astounded at a suggestion of public monies straying. 'Everybody has always...' The Père Sorel still owns the sawmill, and Monsieur Valenod does nicely with the local contractors. Only in very recent years have nosy judges begun to poke into whitewashed accounts and padded invoices. One or two deeply respected old gentlemen have been sent to prison and a couple more have fled the country, but nobody supposes that corruption has been seriously intimidated.

Our village is still an enclave within these wider networks: there is still the feeling that it remains outside the march of material sophistication and prosperity, in their more disagreeable aspects. We have no poor, or not so as you'd notice. No Arabs, Africans or other dispossessed. (There is a disquieting rumour that among us is a Communist voter. I sincerely doubt whether there'd be a single Green vote. We don't lack for Fascists but that we share with all of Alsace/Lorraine.)

Nor have we any rich. Outwardly, every sign of flourishing undertakings. Upon these simple old houses broke out a rash of fanciful ironwork upon window and balcony, greatly admired and much copied. Barns have all become garages and satellite aerials gawk upon every roof; faded stucco walls are repainted in violent chemical colours; we have pavements and gutters in cast concrete, and a grand new bulldozer to clear snow. Roads have been made, and widened. There are street lamps, to a preposterous *belle-époque* pattern; much tinkering with cables and conduits. The crooked and dangerous debouchment upon the main road has been lavishly roundabouted and one will not be surprised to see traffic-lights appear. Following Celts, Romans, Gauls – and the troops of both the Kaiser and the Führer – an invasion of garden dwarfs threatens. The mayor indeed, a zealous soul, succeeds in his ambition to make Grandfontaine into a tidy dormitory suburb.

Inwardly, how much has changed? This aligned and mechanized orderliness, in the worst possible taste, sits ill upon a Vosges village. Some, evilly inclined, persist in eccentricity, in the French love of junkyard scrap 'too good to throw away', of dingy shutters unpainted in three generations and nettles growing rank where the pot was always emptied. Faint notions persist of a lawless outpost, of an old independence refusing to be assimilated into either France or Germany; a folk-memory perhaps of the Princedom of Salm. Thirty years ago in the pub one still heard the patois spoken. Visitors even only from Strasbourg exclaimed cheerfully: 'It's the far side of the moon' – demanding a large drink in reward for daring. We ourselves, driving out at night in the cold clear stillness, paused a moment in the roadway to scent the wood-smoke and wet spruce foliage; the tree drawn and painted by Dürer (it's in the British Museum). After a moment the eye learned to distinguish the outline of the hills, under thin starlight.

The twentieth century, and my own life, finishes here in a village of polite bogus-countrified suburbia? For Strasbourg itself, the little European city where Goethe was a student and Dürer a journeyman, and which still keeps a medieval and Renaissance memory, sprawls out now far enough to touch us. Another ten – twenty – years and the old stone *fermette* will be a desirable residence: will the cowslips and the wood anemones come every spring to my meadow?

9

VILLAGE TECHNIQUES

GRANDFONTAINE and the woodsmen are symbiotic. Even today, when a man might well find his daily work as far off as Strasbourg, and his wife has her own car and job, there are families – dynasties – of professional woodcutters, and they are our aristocracy. The man adumbrated has a little tractor in his garage; for his small son, playing outside, the first and most important toy is a tractor. Wood is in their blood. This man does not want oil to heat his house: it stinks. In the long summer days very early in the morning I hear him rumble past: riding the trailer behind is the little boy, now eight years old and able to help his father in the year's most important chore. They are going into the woods to *faire le bois*. Trunks and branches, sawed to six-foot lengths, are hauled home and stacked to weather, at least a year before they are needed. When this is done they will cut and split last year's wood to billets, and the women of the house will pile it neat and ready for use. A wearisome task? At the very least hard labour over three, four weekends. Nobody will complain of it. *Faire le bois* comes as natural as breathing. These trees were cut the winter before, when the sap was no longer rising, left in the woods until now, stripped of their bark, marked with the man's initials in bright aerosol colour to show his ownership. The professionals have kept back a few beeches for domestic use. For them the chore is not worth comment.

The woods which enclose Grandfontaine upon every side are for the most part state forest, the largest in Europe (we have not yet grown used to thinking of Finland and Sweden as 'ours'). It runs even today for long miles unbroken and one can readily get lost in it. From time out of mind village commithes had rights in it, and some is still private property, but in general the state forester is sole authority over what may be cut; marking and reserving sectors for preservation or regeneration; experimenting with different and new essences (to use a graphic and beautiful French word), planting and cherishing. Around this village there are five of them, living in houses (many old and splendid) provided by the administration, answering to a chief, eventually to 'The Engineer' in Schirmeck, to high and shadowy authority in Strasbourg or Nancy. The department of Les Eaux et Forêts is a very mighty, very French piece of government. The German *Jägermeister* is better trained to scientific higher standards, but the French forester is no longer a peasant with the *képi* of officialdom; he is biologist and entomologist; he preserves rare plants, birds and beasts; he controls and culls the ever-menacing deer, and upon him rests the responsibility for what still remains of the planet's natural coverage. It's not at all exaggerated to say that our civilization stands or falls by his energy and intelligence. The village, by definition obdurate to administrative constraint, does not carry him in their heart. For even the professional woodcutters may not budge save with his permission and under his authority.

The professional also passes my door. This is the immense monster – the familiar of Oregon or Vancouver, whose claw takes hold of a thirty-metre trunk and shakes it, as a terrier would a rat.

When it comes down the road the windows shake; the metre-thick stonework of the house trembles. It is like the ogre, in the Märchen, snoring after a heavy meal. The deep grumble is heard five minutes off. Loaded, the articulated trailer passes me at slow marching pace. In Märchen the little boy peers at the ogre, wondering how many children will be put on the spit to roast for supper. I peer with terror at the ogre. It could deforest France in the time it would take me to read the weekend edition of the *New York Times*.

The professionals like to show the traditional skills of their antique craft. They come, sometimes from all over Europe, to compete in the fine points of axemanship. Locally, no mid-summer fair would be complete without a demonstration of skill and speed. In pioneer North America the backwoods-man (the term is now an insult) could build a house of close-fitting joinery, tenoned and morticed, with the axe alone. Remnants of this survive in the shaping and laying of a delicate ten-metre Eiffel Tower – the sacred midsummer fire built by every Vosges village on St John's Eve; a ritual pre-Christian, and long before that ... Here, in practically every garden, stands an example of woodcutter's art, the figure of bird or deer chipped from a stump: will one laugh? One would be wrong: of the same origins come the limewood Renaissance altar-pieces as well as cuckoo-clock art.

The same skill, the same respect, made the haulage paths carved into the hillsides; concentric circles like a spiderweb, fitted to the contours, in gradients suited to the patient team of horse or mule. They are very old, carpeted with leaf-mould. Mosses and the fluid, hair-fine mountain grass line the verges. One found orchises and seedlings which crushed by a heavy boot grew into bonsais. Channels of split logs drained the many tiny springs. Mushrooms grew in shadow, bilberries in the sunny openings. An old root laid bare, a boulder set aside, a hollow of fine red sand, made a Japanese alcove of worship. Between the trees grew plumes of grass and heather. Seepage made for boggy patches with a half-dozen sorts of fern, and insect-eating flowers. So that I recall and celebrate the joy with which we walked these paths. One might – did – stumble upon one long abandoned, with fallen rocks and rotted trees athwart. Often we tried to lift a plant, but taken from their habitat they sicken and soon die ...

Along these heights one came everywhere upon the traces of 1914: bunker and casemate and gun-emplacement, works of might and cunning but deep-sunk under only fifty years (the work of the forest is ruthlessly rapid) of wind and rain. There is no room for sentiment; golden grove-unleaving pays little heed to Margaret-grieving. Down towards the village we will find a – touching? – recollection of some cottage. A square of foundation dug; a field to be recognized by a crumble of drystone-walling. A cherry tree run wild, and a little spring of water lipping over a stone cut by a man ...

Some of these paths could still be followed. They have been brutally widened for the bulk and tonnage of today's machinery. On the steeper slopes the massive caterpillar-tracked engines have mounted roaring, belching diesel exhaust, crushing mossy stumps. The churned earth shows a huge raw scar in the naked subsoil, boulders flung aside, all growth obliterated. The weight of engines has impacted the woodway into vile ruts where the rain-water cannot drain, and lies black and oily.

A wasteful power; a sickening indiscriminate greed. Honest trees of mature growth have been snapped and flung away to sprawl and rot. The sawmill wants only the biggest and choicest.

'*Nous n'irons plus aux bois.*'

So I mutter, in a small still voice.

'But it's only a very small area,' said the forester.

'True. So was Passchendaele.'

'What? ... Where's that?' And if I sat, I suppose, in an office (air-conditioned, a hundred stories up, in the Mitsubishi Tower), pointed my finger at the atlas, Insulinde, lot of silly little islands, uh, Bali-Timor-Flores, he too would say 'Very small'. Viewed from the satellite, Amazonia too: very small.

One is often reminded of the student, in the Conrad book, who has betrayed his friend to the secret police, and who shouts at the judge in his ecstasy of despair and disgust and self-hatred –

'I resign, I abdicate, I renounce. I withdraw...'

'Yes?' says the judge soft-voiced. 'Where to?'

Some years ago, in Grandfontaine, the woodsmen loaded a big trunk. A bearded, sacking-aproned man cracked a whip and the powerful horses began to move the timbertug down-hill. It was before my time but I can read it in Kipling, see it with those magical eyes. The *Puck* stories that he wrote for his children are delicate Victorian water-colours, have faded just a little but, as he himself remarks, he wrote in many layers, and under the surface is hard bone.

Here in the Vosges, where the slopes are steeper than in the weald of Sussex, a technique existed for bringing home the lopped branches. These were loaded on to the *Schlitt* and a direct – dangerous – path taken down the hill.

A *Schlitt* was in concept a sleigh, the runners set wide for stability, with a high curved front bow to contain the load. They were of different sizes; small, one-man jobs and quite large, highly sophisticated, articulated for manoeuvre, with steering and braking mechanisms, calling for three strong and skilled men. One can see them still, kept in barns as souvenirs. Tricky work and to our eye hair-raising. 'Schlittage' was a skill learned in boyhood.

Another classic technique was rafting. On this side of the watershed the brooks were too shallow and twisting. But on the Donon's northeastern 'Lorraine' face are two fair-sized streams. The Saar Rouge and the Saar Blanche become a river while still in France, crosses the border in the noble town of Saarbrücken. The Saar joins the Mosel (yes, quite right, steep gorges, the Moselle vineyards) at the old Roman fortress of Trier. And together the waters rush on down to join with the Rhine at Koblenz. It would indeed have been possible to pole rafts of logwood downstream, though surely not from here, where the brooks are too shallow. Interesting lesson in politics, since rivers have no nationalist sentiments: one recalls Pascal's remark that truth, on this side of the Pyrenees, is heresy on the other. We had a hilarious illustra-tion of this when the radioactive cloud from the Chernobyl disaster covered Europe. Among other German precautions taken was an interdict on salad plants, which were on sale freely in Strasbourg; France having simply announced that there was no cloud. It was clearly to be understood that the majesty of the Republic had put a stop to all fall-out in the exact centre of the Rhine.

A third technique belonged to the village, was indeed exclusive to Grandfontaine, and was the most imaginative of all; a tiny railway invented during the German rule and thus called the Waldbahn. It was a great success and people came from all over Europe to study its workings: it would have been widely copied were it not for the Great War. Based on a cheap and simple method of laying and joining rails, it crept through our valleys and down to the sawmill at Schirmeck. Most of it was single-track but switches and sidings allowed empty trains going up to pass the loaded wagons going down. It acquired further branches. On the way up to the high woods it climbed a sharp and steep curve: there is a photo of hitherto sceptical notables applauding as it puffed gallantly past. In these old sepia photographs it looks like a fascinating toy, but the little puffing engines could haul wood quicker and cheaper than any other method. Plans were set afoot to extend it into the Donon massif: by 1916 it had reached the village centre, and from there an ingenious aerial cable ferried supplies to the soldiers. One photo shows the Kronprinz and even the Kaiser here on the platform, expressing warm approval.

From Schirmeck in the valley to the plateau named the Col de Praye it covered some twenty-five kilometres. Some confusion and more embarrassment surrounds its pulling down. One may suspect France of a vengeful frame of mind after 1918: a wish hastily to rub out traces of the German administration. There were more examples of this, and more again after 1945. Too many people for comfort had collaborated over-enthusiastically with the occupying power, had done too well out of it. A good deal of righteous indignation was the order of the day, as is very understandable, as is also usual. Those who had been subservient were so still, discreet about their doings and their bank accounts.

One could not possibly wish to keep any physical trace of the Hitler regime. In Schirmeck there was a nasty little prison which has been razed totally, with the hope that the local people who had staffed it would also be forgotten. Signs of the Kaiser's days (which lasted fifty years) persist. Even now there are bits of social legislation applicable in Alsace and Lorraine, plainly more just towards the working people than that of the rest of France.

One can still follow stretches of the paths built for the Waldbahn. They are as striking as any of the Grandfontaine ghosts. And in the village pieces of looted rail keep stacked firewood from the damp ground.

Earlier in these pages I made mention of the orientation table on the top of the Donon mountain. Placed there by the Kaiser's surveyors to celebrate the acquisition to the Reich of two beautiful provinces: a massive bronze compass rose embellished in gothic lettering with helpful information. It enchanted me that the arrow pointing northeast says 'Saint Petersburg' and the southwesterly with equal splendour 'Madrid'. The view here is incomparable and the vision Napoleonic. Others and of the same facture were certainly planted at strategic outposts of the Imperium, designed and forged by the same firm. On the island of Norderney, in the North Sea (then pompously termed the German Ocean and we know from the *Riddle of the Sands* that here too the Kaiser liked to cast his eye afar) I found an identical table, with a southwesterly arrow pointing boldly to 'The Donon'.

What kind of witness do I make, of my own Europeanness? I can quote Crèvecoeur, a French writer who was also soldier and farmer, who emigrated to America, lived through both revolutions, and is here writing in 1782.

> I could point out to you a family whose grandfather was an Englishman whose wife was Dutch; whose son married a Frenchwoman; whose present four sons have now four wives of different nations.

He is an American, who leaving behind him all his ancient prejudices and manners, receives new ones from the new mode of life he has embraced, the new government he obeys, and the new rank he holds.

Well now; making allowances for the French love of rhetoric, for – in translation – his shaky syntax (Tocqueville is the better writer), this is a remarkably accurate picture of myself. I can laugh; a couple of generations ago like other Freelings I could no doubt have chosen to be American . . .

Surely this is the gift to me of Grandfontaine, to have forged me into a European.

One could find counterparts anywhere one looks, of this Vosges village, obstinately itself and refusing still to be either French or German. Northern Italy even today so Austrian; Sudeten Czechs; Hungarian Slovaks; Silesian Poland and even now East Prussia. Almost all indeed of European Russia. The wretched tales today of Bosnia and Herzegovina; the saving of Sarajevo is to recognize itself a European city.

I was brought here: I have come for a purpose.

10

VICTUALLING

A WRITER BREATHES IN WORDS as he does oxygen, and the child notices them: 'In the Beginning was the Word' comes naturally and gets taken literally. As soon as it can read it studies the odd phrases on notice-boards (with a liking for the peremptory. 'Warning: One Train Can Conceal Another' is an incantation). Shopfronts, in the England of the 1930s, were a potent source. 'Wm. Jackson, Licenced Grocer and Victualler.' (What was 'Wm.'?) 'Well,' said my father 'you know the French word *ravitaillement*.' Vittles were plainly vital: ships also got revictualled.

The English have always been odd about their vittles; make a fuss nowadays about food but one suspects this to be a passing fashion because it has never much interested them. The French traditionally were good at the making, cooking, eating of it. Is it also a passing fashion to pretend, as they do, that they've no time for it? Terrible fast-food proliferates even in the countrysides; the taking of pains has become tiresome.

In the Vosges villages this appears more natural; the *ravitaillement* is not a complicated matter. The ground is poor. At this altitude grapes will not ripen and tomatoes only in a good year. People ate heartily since heavy work calls for it but the victuals were rough and monotonous. Their habits have changed little over the last fifty years. They spend more but take reluctantly to the unfamiliar.

Plenty of cabbage and potatoes; onions and leeks; apples, cherries, plums. There was not a lot of butter and oddly little cheese. Except for smoked and salted pork, meat was seldom seen and fish scarcely at all (the brook trout were plentiful but small and bony). A chicken or a rabbit was a feast-day dish, and white flour was expensive, so that cakes were few.

The wild resources were strangely little used, save mushrooms (the woods are full of *cèpes*). The ever-present deer and wild pig, staple of all Europe, but with no great enthusiasm. Wild fruit too was oddly disregarded. The meadows are full of strawberries, the wood verges a tangle of raspberry and bramble, but only the lovely forest bilberries, *les myrtilles*, seem prized, and bushes of black- and redcurrants left to birds. Perhaps sugar was unduly expensive. Many villagers kept bees.

A good gardener had carrots and salads. The prudent housewife cherished her broody hen, guarded the chickies from fox and hawk. She had milk to put on the children's porridge, and dripping from the pig; she had little butter and no oil.

If one compares this world with Ireland (where the climate is mild and the poor thrived, if only on potatoes) – or with the harsh southern coasts (they have cheese, salt fish, the odd goat, but above all they have olives, and olives are vital) – one can say that hereabouts they didn't do badly. The woodcutter (a charcoal burner was in the forest for a week on end) took bacon with him, hacked off a slice with the pocketknife, grilled it speared on a stick, and baked potatoes in the embers: in the English forests of Dean or Sherwood it can have been no different.

When he got home, what had the good-wife cooked? The Bäckeofen, traditional dish of the Vosges; the earthenware pot. She put in a few morsels of meat; the restaurant version calls for a piece of beef and of mutton as well as pork. She filled the pot with leeks, onions, and plenty of potatoes; she moistened it with cheap white wine – coming as it did from nearby Alsace this was never dear. She sealed the lid (that is the secret) with flour paste so that the juices would not evaporate. She put her pot in the oven of her stove which overnight burns low, and left it there twelve hours. This is a splendid dish. I can remark that the famous and beautiful peasant dishes of France are all made the same way. The cassoulet, the *daube* or the Gascon stew. Time, care, love, a low oven. All of them qualities now largely evaporated but which still exist. Being poor you have not much meat. You don't need much since the flavour impregnates the whole. I suppose that in its origins the Lancashire hotpot was not much different. For in central Europe (of which Lancashire forms part) the stove burns the year round.

Along the Mediterranean coasts the housewife has not the vital (victual) resource of the fire which in Grandfontaine burns through even the summer day. So that she brought her pot to the baker: his oven (dying down once his bread was done) accommodated twenty village pots. Hence the homely southern dish still called 'Boulanger' even if we have forgotten how it was made.

The other universal dish of this world is *la choucroute*. An essential prop: the round and dense autumn cabbage when salted and fermented will nourish the poorest for a twelve-month, until the next year's harvest. The chemistry of this preserves all the minerals and vitamins that even a growing child will need. It is a simple chemistry and was done at home: for the cities, little factories mechanized the process. Sliced fine with a knife the cabbage was put in a barrel, flavoured with peppercorns and juniper berries, and salt added. Heavy weights press down the lid; the rising scum and liquid is discarded. When fermentation ends (a few weeks) it will keep (kept cool). It will be abundantly rinsed in fresh water before use. Sauerkraut.

An odd paradox applies here. This dish is an essential prop in the victualling of central Europe. Since it keeps over the winter months, at a pinch even until next year's harvest, you would expect it to be a great standby wherever the ground is poor, as well as in the industrial areas. So it is, all across temperate – meaning cabbage – Europe; the process does not lessen the minerals and vitamin values. But in opulent Alsace, barn and storehouse for less favoured areas, for the *loess* of the Rhine valley is wonderful farming ground, they'll eat this dish several times a week, with the greatest possible enthusiasm.

There is a phenomenon too, for which I have never found an explanation to really satisfy me: the people of the British islands do not eat sour cabbage. The idea seems never to have occurred to them. One of their Apartheid notions; for years the word *Kraut* was a term of opprobrium, hurled at the peoples of Germany. It is the odder since these island peoples were chronically badly fed. Just how bad this was, anyone of my age can remember vividly. The odder still since in Denmark or Holland, maritime countries, the dish is known and welcomed. There are a lot more Brit oddities difficult to fathom but this is not the smallest.

Can one make a distinction between people interested in food and those who aren't? I should think it could only be made individually – the French have the reputation of connoisseurs, which is greatly exaggerated and largely mythical; it is like saying that Germans are all musical. A parsimonious and avaricious people, they became skilled at making a lot out of a little. So did the Chinese the other country famous for ingenuity and variety of cooking. Looking at France (which to me comes naturally since I live there) one will find a lot more paradoxical observations.

In Alsace, for instance – they remain an obstinately Germanic folk but after three hundred years under the French umbrella they are imbued with Gallic patterns – one eats strangely badly. The *charcuterie* (generic name for the pork-butcher's product) is of poor quality, and the traditional accompaniment to the *choucroute*, at least five varieties of smoked and salted pork and sausage, is quantitavely impressive but too often of disgustingly poor quality – one need only cross the Rhine to find much better. They don't understand ham ... This is very odd; ham after all can be famous anywhere in Europe. Count on your fingers very quickly. Prague and Westphalia; the Ardennes; Parma and Bayonne (and a half-dozen famous addresses in Spain). While here it is revolting; a leg of pig injected with salt water, cut thick and thrown at you; tough, watery, tasteless ... what the hell is the matter with them? (And all too often the same will be put on your plate in Paris.)

One will begin to say 'Aha' after noticing that all over France butchers' meat is a misery, be it pork, beef, veal or lamb; anything eatable will be an eye-opening rarity. There is to be sure a simple explanation of this nasty phenomenon. Butchers, like pharmacies or the notorious funeral enterprises, are a very well-protected species, quite shameless in their naked pursuit of ever-greater profits. In the interest of this all-conquering instinct, they sell meat far too fresh: since they sell by weight the profit is in the water. Simple; when meat is hung until tender, and the evaporation has concentrated the juices, you have lost ten per cent of the wet weight at slaughter ... no butcher can bear to lose this heavy slice of pure profit on which he pays no taxes. You pay; you are paying for the water.

But, you will say, surely the customer objects? It is one of the stupefying truths of France – the customer doesn't have a clue, thinks that all meat is like this. In the United States, where one can see meat ripening, where a steak is sacred, he would be perplexed. One can eat well, still, here in Alsace? Upon occasion, as in the rest of France; it becomes a rarity. The food is complicated, the expense exorbitant, the pleasure much mitigated. A famous critic (it was Curnonsky) said that the finest dish he knew was a soft-boiled egg. The simplicity of good food is a truth now widely forgotten. A cook's skill is learned but his taste is inborn. Cooks, like gardeners, have an instinct, without knowing too much about the how or the why.

I think it will be fair to say that one is much likelier to find a good glass of wine. The Alsace vineyard, long despised and dismissed as a source of cheap plonk, abounds in delight: in the unassuming cellars of foothill farms are amazing glories. Widely varied growths, delicate and sensitive, so that one tastes widely, will fall readily into the absurdities of the professional jargon.

Will we drink wine in heaven? We presume perhaps over-hastily that we won't, that we are then detached from carnal pleasures. I am not convinced that these pleasures are merely carnal – the word is pejorative. Our imagination is so limited, our senses so narrow and enfeebled. Hereabouts, already, the surprises are great and sudden. I suspect there will be many more, which Brother Ass[5] cannot envisage, could not encom-pass. Where art is concerned, anything is possible. We have sometimes glimpsed extraordinary things through keyholes.

I should like to find myself in our snow-bound Vosges woods. I am sitting on the back of my legs (which I no longer can) since the floor of the forest is wet. I have made a fire. The sticks hiss for they were powdered with snow. They spit, for they are mostly old conifer branches. A flicker runs along the branch, bright blue – and emerald green. A feath-ery silver ash falls into orange embers. Fire is elemental so that this is primitive, a concentrate of metaphysics. There are also stones, trees, earth (a scrape of pure leaf-mould); water is nearby. I am holding a sharpened stick on which I am grilling a piece of dry smoke-blackened bacon. I should hope that also, standing in the snow, is a bottle of Alsace wine. In a trouser pocket is the Laguiole knife; a blade, a marlinspike, and a corkscrew. In the jacket pocket – I greatly hope – is a piece of black Russian bread. I am as close to God as I will get, for a little while still.

'Why can we not fly?' asked Mr Chadband. 'No wings,' suggested Mr Snagsby, who is always ready to be helpful; to the displeasure of all present. But of course I can fly: by simply lighting a cigarette I can be standing in the Mauritshuis, a formal, elegant town-house, not quite a palace, in The Hague. I am standing in the room sacred above all others because I am looking at the *View of Delft*, and if I were

---

5. Francis of Assisi's bleak but affectionate and never contemptuous term for his own body.

to turn right about – as I will in my good time – on the opposite wall a girl's head by Vermeer is looking at me.

Or – I could be in another room; small, dark, silent. In Madrid; looking at me is the little Infanta, and her dwarfs; and in the corner that is Velázquez, painting the eyes of the world. Innocence and knowledge and sorrow: one cannot endure this sight for more than a few minutes, but one will always come back. Or music will do it just as well.

That the village isn't important – is that what you're saying? That imagination will allow you to be anywhere and that thus it doesn't matter ... No. Young men often think like this and so did I as a boy 'with a heart of furious fancies'. Through adolescence and into maturity the imagination is so powerful: the boy is much impressed by it, especially if, as I was, he is weak-muscled, lacking in endurance, woefully short of physical energy.

A reader of my generation might remember (since in age the memory for childhood becomes magical) the comics of pre-war days, and the 'Charles Atlas' advertisements. There were two pictures side by side, one of a scrawny boy – 'are you a puny weakling?' – the other flexing mighty muscles and a smirk to go with them – 'you too can be like this'. I did not envy Charles Atlas, who looked a bit thick, though I was mightily envious of boys who could run and swim, but I made do with my own powers, which I could switch on. They are rather similar to physical strength and can be impressive until in adulthood one learns that none of these talents are of themselves anything much. The greatest of athletes falls early enough among thieves. But one struts about awhile, pleased with oneself.

People who have lost their home (fleeing the Red Army, I suppose, the most numerous in my day) have earned all the sympathy they can get. Those who have never had any home that they can remember have to build one. They have no time to waste on self-pity. My own discovery, that nowhere was there a place I could call mine (most certainly do I refuse to blame either my parents or myself), came late. For many years imagination pictured greener fields just around the corner. Once (there is no self-pity but is it self-indulgent to mention it?) I found a wonderful house. Like Madame Verdurin's 'Raspelière', with the three views. Once I was on the verge of buying land, spent three glowing days designing the house I would build. On both occasions some instinct forced me to swerve away, at the last moment. And this house, which is now ours and which instinct did not block, would in the eyes of the world be worthless. We have a couple of acres of steep hill ground, which one has to climb, to have a view. Now that the trees on the southern crest have grown we have not even sunlight through the winter months. The house itself left always much to be desired. Oh well, we got it cheap. The climate is harsh. The children take an indulgent view of 'Dad's Folly'. What will they do with it when I no longer stand around haunting? Ridiculous, preposterous: twenty times we have tried to leave, swearing we would never come back. Yes, it is an interesting spot. At some length I have tried to spell out why. Geography: if there is a centre of our little European peninsula, the near-island, it is here. History – I have sketched some of the reasons for the strategic position of the village. My own restless, silly, nonsensical span of years; over seventy now but how long will that be prolonged? But it was, is, a personal equation, and to bring the two sides to meet in the = , the equality symbol of resolution, disentanglement; that is the task of this book.

There is still something to come. Like Proust in the notorious cork-lined room I am alone with my book. He had got rid of the world. The last room in the rue Hamelin was by all accounts bleak and uninviting, to anyone but himself (and Celeste) horrible. 'Celeste, will we ever write the word "End" to our book?' It was hers too, by then. He was Charles Atlas; his muscles are enviable. But I have begun to understand.

Nothing is easy in this scrap of the European heartland, and never was. Nothing, ever, came easy to the people here.

A dour hardy folk, none too ready to speak or smile. No languor; nothing smooth or supple, nothing facile. There is no softness in the air; summers and winters are harsh, for we are far from the sea. The northerly is to be dreaded, a fierce polar air which blows a week on end, oppressing the spirit. From the east comes the bear's weather, frank and open, of great beauty, a Russian air. Rarely, the southerly, and when it ceases you can write on the car windscreen in the Sahara sand. But for three days in the five it is the westerly that takes charge, a breath of the Atlantic. We do not know storms here, since the kindly Vosges give shelter, but the rain we know in every tint and tone. Colour, saturated in water particles as fine as the sand – suspended in every handful of the trembling air – filters across the eye; supple and sliding. The greens and blues are those of Ireland, the yellows of springtime petal-fragile. The meteorologists, comic appellation for those who study weather, have tried very hard to distinguish between southern and northern patterns; they have tried to draw a line. It runs just here. By birth, blood, genes, inclination. I have no pull towards southerly shores; I am no bourgeois like Eliot to say 'we read, and go south in the winter'. I belong here.

Good, then, to stand in the flicker of March sunlight and get the stinging bucketful in the face. Good even when the May hail smashes the flowers: 'this year there will be no cherries', while on the foothills between us and the fat farmers of Alsace, vinegrowers mutter at *la coulée* which can destroy the setting grapes just at their most vulnerable: it will be a poor vintage.

But there will be the years when the October sunlight goes on and on, and they will pick the last grapes for Eiswein in November, trudging with the baskets over the blanket of the first feathery snowfall.

At this height we have no grapes. But our thin, acid soil is generous towards maples: they flame in October as in Vermont, scarlet and carmine, orange and crimson, the most anaemic of pale yellow and the most robust muscular bronze. The winter, and as in Vermont, we will hibernate. The time for reading, for music, and – yes, exactly; this is sentimentalism, excruciatingly so. I have read of a writer who has lived for more than thirty winters in rural Vermont, without electricity, and is lyrical about this. The food is probably better than here, but not much. It would be important to me. It's even part of art. Proust knew this, and dining with Saint-Loup in the Rivebelle restaurant notices the chocolate soufflé, boiled potatoes, and Pauillac lamb – the order is strange but he wasn't composing a menu. There is more to food than eating it.

In grand restaurants, where I sometimes worked, we never ate much – a mouthful of salad, of spaghetti. We didn't have time? We were disgusted? More that there is another set of values. We would say 'That's a really pretty turbot' or 'What a lovely sweetbread'. (Neither would be called attractive in any conventional sense.) A sauce, technically, is a juice reduced; we thought in terms of colour and consistency, the perfume, the sheen upon it. It would be eaten, but that was unimportant. Indeed my first chef (in the larder, where raw material is prepared) used to complain that 'We do beautiful work and then the kitchen makes shit of it'. While out there in the dining-room were people who actually ate it, but they were of no interest.

Those people; our jobs depended on them; to please them was our pain and our privilege. (They complained all the time but that was for headwaiters to handle.) Our allegiance was to the turbot, not to those rich enough to eat it. How often I have heard said 'It should be looked at, smelt – and thrown away'.

But later in my life I found myself also a customer, and remembered that in childhood I had loved eating. Writers get taken to lunch, often in splendid establishments, vanity and snobbery playing the role they do in all commerce. I disliked these occasions. I'd rather be alone; concentrate upon what I eat. Company, which is often very good, demands the whole of attention. Then I do not notice what is on my plate; a pity. Only when the companion is as greedy as myself (the place for business is the office) is there enjoyment. And then – the vice of gluttony is always disgusting? A solitary meal is masturbation? Come – the word 'banquet' has metaphysical extensions, and so has the beautiful chemistry of food.

Aesthetics has so much to do with art. The commonest artistic heresy is to think it only a set of aesthetic values (as my larder chef, a man with a strong visual sense, feigned to believe: he knew better of course...). Does the cutter of diamonds think only of giving his stone the maximum brilliance? This will do well in a rose. That insists upon a pear cut. (This here has a flaw and I must think how best to...) The jeweller thinks of mounting it. Does he keep at the front of his mind a woman's skin? Stones lose their lustre in the vaults of banks. The royal crowns, the tiaras of scrawny grannies, are so much dreck. Jewels are for shimmering young girls – or for very old prophets. A dodgy affair, art.

Food; diamonds: merely material chemistry and never art? But art is at the cradle of manufacture.

Painters have often no interest in how it will look in a room, hanging on the wall. The writer too is mired in the mechanics. His book, printed, bound, might also deserve to be handled, smelt, studied and enjoyed: that happens seldom, since publishers see it as just another cornflakes packet. Is there any art, there? The writer; perhaps he prays that some day, in an obscure corner of the sixpenny remainder shelf, a real reader will pick it up and – it may be – find himself in whatever way enlarged by it. That, then, would be art.

Perhaps the musician, now and again? It was technically 'a bad concert'? But something hung a moment on the air, saturating the atmosphere. Then it was gone forever.

No! In metaphysics nothing is lost. Art is forever eternal. We know nothing about God, and precious little about the soul. But art is God's gift to us – perhaps there was a whisper at the cradle, from the *Fée*, into the baby's ear. For in myth we find truths. Art exists in chemistry and in biology; in physics and in mathematics. But the battle to catch hold, to grasp and apprehend, will take every scrap of energy we possess.

I have felt, most bitterly,a lifelong lack of physical energy. It was in mastering this that Proust showed what we call genius. Art springs from the nape of the neck. I found myself battered breathless. But there is no room in art for self-pity.

The village, initially, was a place to take breath in. But if breath failed – was it then a place given one, to make use of?

I am trying, since this is given me, to understand something about art. Which is all we have, here, of God. Possibly, the village is a good place. It has always known how to get rid of the inessential.

I wish to study where this may lead me.

PART THREE

I

A House

THE VILLAGE HAS SHRUNK, a waterspill on hot metal. When I first wrote about it, a few years ago, the walking habit was strong in me and daily I toured about: it was clear I think that the village is not large but straggled widely. I climbed the hills and followed the spider-web woodcutters' paths. From viewpoints that had often in the past been observation posts for artillery the perspective was aerial. Readily one could imagine oneself the bird characteristic of this country: the sailing slow-wheeling buzzard buoyed effortlessly on some unseen thermal. One could smell the woodsmoke. Perhaps I could see (the bird sees the mouse) Bruno outside his back door splitting logs; the thump of his axe reaching me long after the punch of his forearm. Adjusting a hair's breadth, my roof-tops.

This has gone from me. I could say that age, and illnesses have diminished me; I can no longer walk much and then with a stick, heavy and solemn, as though I were doing something important. Vision got narrower as the step came to lumber. The eye takes in no more than the house: I can climb as far as the garden hedge, on the level of my roof-tree.

A romantic fancy; that this was a lighthouse. Grandfontaine, no. 117, but it should have been called *Amer*, the sea-mark. The eye was concerned with soil and what will grow there and with the men and women who work it, but I could lift the eye, see further; as I liked to think right across Europe. Time has passed and a working life, a career, is behind me. What now does it mean, this house, tiny morsel of European ground? What came I here to seek? I have written forty books, half of them here. The Daimon, here in these woods, I know and quite well. That is not easy to speak of.

A fine writer, Mary Renault, put words into the mouth of her 'Theseus' which I cannot better. 'There is something more. What it is I do not know, nor whether there is a name for it. It may be there is some harper, the son and son's son of bards, who knows the word. I only feel it about my heart: it is a brightness, and it is a pain.'

Writers work anywhere; on trains or by the seaside; high in the air. Nathalie Sarraute on tables in the corner of Paris cafés. Some have found houses all-important; Kipling was one. I am another; the source of the brightness and the pain is here around me though I cannot grasp it. There is indeed a name for the thing unknowable; by definition undefinable: metaphysics. We have to start with physical detail because that is all we know.

It's a Vosges farmhouse, quite a good example; an honest, solid look and well-proportioned. An eighteenth-century generosity of doors and windows, the look in England called 'Regency'. Quite right since the date on the stone is 1827. The word sounds odd in rural France. Restauration; fat Louis has recently died and his imbecile brother Charles is about to get the sack. We do not much admire the building style called 'Louis-Philippe' but these village builders worked to the manner of fifty years before and one is very glad of it. A nice house thus, scarcely to be called pretty but with a sober, simple beauty.

The inside is frankly peasant. The rooms, four below and four above, are good-sized and well-lit, but the ceilings are too low, the stairway a narrow ladder, the woodwork a humble deal and there was no bathroom or lavatory: one has to remember that a beautiful palace like vanished Marly had none either. Eighteenth-century sanitation was the china jug and the china pot. The rooms above-stairs were heated by iron stoves with enamelled panels.

Applying oneself to these difficulties took much work and ingenuity. Most of the answers were found in the working half of the house; the stable and carthouse at street level and the barn above that. One wants to – one tries to – respect the character of old houses. An example, the latches of doors and windows, made no doubt by hand in the forge down the road. When they washed, which wasn't often, water was emptied in the Wasserstein, massive piece of local sandstone hollowed into a sort of shallow sink; we have two. Load-bearing walls are a metre thick and to pierce these for piping was not easy. Silver-fish live in the old pine panelling. Electric cable got bundled into corners where many spiders have their being. Several of the beautifully made oak shutters have at last rotted off their hinges. Over a hundred and thirty years the country people put one layer of paint over another, of a pea-green colour.

And in the thirty following, of our time, the village carpenter doubled all twenty windows, replaced the rickety staircase in hardwood ... the boys restuccoed the walls and renewed the roof tiles. They have invested more than anyone. I repapered the rooms, not the simplest of jobs since a village builder in the 1820s worked by eye, and there isn't an exact right angle to be found here. But the work on any old house is a Catalogue of Ships:[6] a prolonged and undeniable bore.

It is a good house for a writer. I have thought, and very often, of Kipling finding Jacobean Batemans down in the valley below Burwash, 'all untouched and unfaked' – yes and both dark and damp. But I understand his great joy, and the love he put into it. The comparison can go no further: he was very rich, very famous and a most marvellous writer. We all do what we can. When I bought this house, for the children when small, it did not occur to me to see it as anything but a change of scene, where after the week's work we could stretch our knees, breathe deeply and smell wood-smoke. It was like any country cottage; we enjoyed the primitive feeling, and getting up early on a Monday morning, sweeping

---

6. A notoriously boring section of the *Iliad*.

snow off the car in the dark to drive the children back to school, was with a sense of refreshment. Wonderful for a Christmas party and the tradition grew up of going into the woods to search out and cut a young fir for 'the tree'.

Perhaps there will be a little more to it than an exercise in simple psychology. There is here a juice, an essence, of all the houses that have gone before. Writing 'The Tale of Anne D.' I gave some weight to the long, sad and comic list of 'Nancy's houses'. There were a good few before I arrived upon the scene, and after I left the maternal clutch: I have maintained – alarmingly – the Freeling vagabondage. Only this house refused to be cut out of our lives. Even when standing empty it kept a magnetism one would almost call malignant, refusing two or three attempts to sell it.

The two French houses of my own early childhood left little trace – nor I believe did the first two English houses, despite vivid memories. The sombre and deep-gripping presence of Bitterne Manor House, a melancholy shot through with many streaks of a nigh unbearable happiness – that does not leave me, never could. The four-square, oddly attractive stone house in a remote Irish village left as I now realize more of a mark than I knew, and so did the flat – sunny, delightful, elegant – in Georgian Dublin, later mirrored in the beautiful Regency house in Brighton where our first child was born. Thereafter four more houses saw a child's birth; one in England, two in Holland, the last here in Strasbourg. Every one would leave an ingredient, just as a perfumer composes a new scent, which would contribute to the atmosphere I breathe at this moment.

We always hear a lot about the English sense of humour, perhaps rather too much; they insist so fiercely that nobody else has any, one begins to wonder about theirs. There is a lot of prate about heavy Germans (always then known as Teutons), solemn Spanish, frivolous but unfunny French, and so on: it is part of the terrifying English xenophobia, which itself is part of the particular English terror; that perhaps after all they aren't the chosen people. By dint of always insisting on being first (and the rest nowhere) they become absurd figures of fun. They wield – though – irony better than most; isn't this the mainspring of their laughter? If we forget how to laugh at ourselves we're in a bad way?

I am a ludicrous figure; not especially so; no more really, I suppose, than everyone. Less certainly than politicians and a lot more people who come readily to mind. It is needful to find myself and remind myself that I am a figure of fun; one becomes very solemn. I get old, have too often been ill, suffer a lot of pain and I'm afraid I'm humourless about it all. Perhaps the best English joke and probably the best-known is the antique wisecrack about 'Does it Hurt?' – 'Only when I laugh . . .'

The house is as ludicrous as myself. Everyone agrees it's an awful house and the word 'horrible' has been used, quite justly. Dark, damp, badly sited, jammed into that beastly hill-side, and we only get six months of real sun in the twelve: I must have been out of my mind then and certainly am so now. Why did we never make up our minds once and for all to be rid of it? We wouldn't have made any money but it wouldn't have cost much either. This last long while – a good fifteen years – all I have done is to wedge myself further in. There was that marvellous house which we *just* didn't buy (with the three views, like Madame Verdurin's 'Raspelière'). There was the moment when I found an exceptional terrain, only one view but that magnificent, of mountain, sea, and Atlantic sunset. The farmer, a gentle, true and ungreedy man, had no real use for it and was ready to let it go for peppercorns. We had a verbal agreement. The builder had measured the foundation and I had drawn both plan and elevation. Is it merely pathetic or is it the more laughable that I turned tail and fled? Yes, I do quite often have night-mares about these moments, finding them unfunny.

I think the truth is that this house contains more than real houses of the years past; also fictional houses known and loved. This is still quite simple psychology, not yet metaphysics.

Primo Levi, the Man, a splendid and greatly gifted man, remarked that he found writing surprisingly easy and thought it likely that this was due to his training as a chemist. For the writer was concerned with filtering, with crystallizing, with distilling; chemists' jobs of which he had much experience. There is plenty of truth in this as in most things he says, and perhaps also it is a little too precise, exact, mechanical: these artistic functions (in my experience, I should guess that of others of more talent) are not clean-cut. In manipulations the chemist's hand does not tremble. The artist – I am citing Kipling – can sometimes recognize the presence of the Daimon. Speaking for himself the moments before dawn were the most propitious, with a south-west wind blowing. Grandfontaine, tucked under the easterly lip of the Vosges, in a narrow glen or dale protected on all sides but the east by thick woods, does not know the wind. It can blow a gale in many houses I have lived in.

'Schele Jaapie klim de mast – cross-eyed Jackie hold fast. (The Dutch are given to little rhymes.) Nostalgia calls up houses which creak and sway. A gale blowing on the coast, as children we were brought up to pray for the sailors; in these Breton villages one woman in two was a widow. We invoked the protection of the Lady, the Stella Maris, and perhaps here we learned the first lesson; that the world is utterly ruthless and the ways of God are inscrutable. Prayer isn't enough. The waves can reach the lantern of the lighthouse. In Grandfontaine there are other kinds of wind, which also have made widows. The people of this house saw the front line in 1914, and in 1940 knew the 'Passeurs' who, risking their own lives, guided refugees upon the woodcutters paths across the frontier.

Layer upon layer, thus, where I began to understand – as I tried to make clear in another part of this book – a thousand years of European history. My personal history is then very unimportant. But the other houses of my past, which have come – comically – to be embodied here, are perhaps a key to metaphysical realities. So too, I think, are the houses of my childhood reading, for to the child imagination has more power than schools, or illnesses, the clothes one wears, the food one eats, the incomprehensible pains in the humdrum of daily existence, of which one cannot speak. A book, even a forgotten piece of Victorian fiction, has life and immense energy for a further unexpected, maybe unmerited span in the mind. I had seen, and would never forget, the lights around Le Croisic, had seen pictures, read descriptions of the building of the Eddystone or Bishop Rock. The word 'lighthouse' came really to life only with a preposterous piece of lurid taletelling such as flourished on every publisher's list at the turn of the century; splendidly titled *The Watchers on the Longships*.

There are more and more obvious sources for this house as it would become for me. The most vigorous is certainly Seekings House, the house made by John Masefield, himself a lonely little boy, for 'Kay Harker'. *The Midnight Folk* is well known as a splendid children's book; must have captivated many, and took total possession of myself aged seven: every page of it, sixty-five years later, vivid and instantly recoverable. The little boy alone in a creaky candle-lit old house full of witches; it tells me a lot about the child I was. Here, reading aloud to my own children, we have often heavy snow and electricity cuts are no surprise: candle-light will supply the witches.

What began as a metaphor has been fortified by circumstances and has hardened into reality: the house is an island. The mainland is not far away and can be reached with an effort; a causeway bare at low tide and slippery with weed, but no; it is real enough, needs no decorating from the ever-ready imagination.

Islands are jokes; look how many cartoonists make drawings of them. The appeal to imagination is indeed constant and universal: people dream of them; millionaires buy them; hermits withdraw to them. They are romance, and they have often been prisons. Some writers' islands have been horridly actual; one thinks of Stevenson working feverishly to support his greedy parasites. Places of desperation, haunting and harsh as in Conrad's *Victory*. Bogus, like Axel Munthe's *San Michele*; wound about with an oddly persistent glamour like Norman Douglas's Capri. Pantomime islands – Peter Pan and Captain Hook. A few years ago a woman called Lucy Irvine had a shot at making the 'coral island' myth come to life, with an exceedingly sour result. The most famous of all, *Treasure Island*, is seen to be a most horrible place, fit for nightmares.

And islands are not jokes at all; dangerous and disturbing, and I am well placed to know it. Their strongest appeal is to the soft-hearted and the soft-headed, people of chronic bad judgement. I know this, since it is exactly my own case.

We live, at the turn of this century, an eruption – a continued series of explosions – of discoveries: there is nothing very new about that, but since the most obvious and omnipresent is the new facility in communications and the instant spread of information we are made aware of discovery, and of every novelty, as never before. An island can do us a good turn here, by slowing down the babble. One has at least a chance to take breath before swallowing whatever we are told. A deal, and a very great deal, of the info isn't fact at all but propaganda. The power of rumour and the malice of gossip are known to us; *suppressio veri* and *suggestio falsi* have been powerful gods since our beginnings.

Is it reasonable to say that mine was the first generation to feel the full force of this? In my childhood the radio, the 'wireless' as we called it, the TSF (*télégraphe sans fil*: words implying a magical, mysterious process) wasn't universal, and certainly not portable; a ponderous and expensive object, a sort of cabinet enthroned in the living-room, often full of static and given to breaking down. There were serious talks, political addresses; there was music-hall entertainment and football matches. Good fun; one didn't have to take it all that seriously. Only with the war, I believe, did it become sanctified – 'Here is the News and this is Jonathan Goodbody reading it' – after the solemn silence and the pips. The people of Europe began to think – indeed to feel total trust – that in the BBC was Truth. The King and Mr Churchill for uplift, Itma for morale, Haw-Haw for a good laugh, but the News for the Gospel, and Jonathan Jesus preaching it. Did it ever occur to us that we heard what they wanted us to hear, believed what they wished us to believe? Scarcely ever. There must have been a few sturdy spirits who sniggered ('One of our aircraft is missing') but to be heard doing so was unpatriotic, risking venomous insult and widespread boycott. The hardest-headed turned into innocents like myself; I have this fatal habit of believing what people tell me – to this day upset when the plumber says 'tomorrow' and never turns up.

Islands are for the vulnerable. You learn quickly, and when some loutish child of seven says 'Miserable little squit, aren't you?' and repartee fails (convinced as you are that it's no more than the truth) an island is desirable, and shortly to become indispensable. Such children are easily flustered, have no quick answer. *Esprit d'escalier*; we think of something witty on our way downstairs. Parents and guardians are likely to say we'll grow out of it. So we do, outwardly; by the time of entering the army I was as robust as any. It was at the price – and this is frequent – of pretending to despise the talents one hasn't got, and I would quickly be known as 'Roger the Dodger': artful type. One begins to confuse acting with reality. When some sergeant screams 'Stand up straight you fucking useless object' – is one deliberately making one shoulder lower than the other? I had thought I truly was standing upright.

On his island Ben Gunn is a great man, until Silver says 'Dead or alive, nobody cares for him' and all his treasure is stolen by the squire and the doctor (thorough bastards both) and he goes home a pathetic nobody. There's nothing he can do with his treasure, nowhere to go with it. Common handicap with islands.

It would be a mistake to interpret this in a narrowly literal sense of isolation in some filtered area – now a commonplace in light industry -where dust is not allowed and to sneeze creates scandal. I have few memories of early childhood in France, and it was twenty years before sounds and smells would suddenly be familiar – the discovery of buried memories is a sentimental journey.

The year was 1931 and the Depression making itself felt. In tracing 'The Tale of Anne D.' I have sketched the restless nature of this woman, her great physical energy and grasshopper impulsiveness as well as – I hope – the tremendous capacity for loving and being loved, the great funniness, the immense charm. As – physically – Walter faded he seems to recede more and more into the background during the eight years he still had to live, while Nancy becomes an ever more bumptious and obstreperous figure until her spectacular collapse.

2

Before the War

Southampton was the nearest point in England to Saint
Malo; the two were linked by ferry. It was also a marker
in Nancy's own youth; her mother had for long lived in the
countryside – leafy and truly rural – close by: I know of no
other reason why we should have settled there. An interesting town, of abrupt and brutal contrasts; inland sleepy and
bourgeois, the dockland area grimy, huddled, slummy. An
old town, with the remnants of a citadel and bits of fortified
wall of great size and strength, built to command the vast
fjord; Southampton Water was much more than an inlet,
and the port's fame rested on the famous double tide of the
Channel water running round both sides of the Isle of
Wight. The docks extended into the black evil-smelling
Totton but inland lay rural Hampshire and the New Forest;
the newish suburbs of Bassett and Swaythling had a clean
and cosy feel. I think I must describe this town in more
detail because it had so much importance in my life during
these years before the Second World War.

One main street ran north and south. From the town
centre (a Victorian clock tower of the usual hideous style)
north along the Avenue, skirting the Common (the English
are happy in these immense green spaces), the University
buildings and bourgeoisdom out along the Winchester road.
To the South a busy shopping street cut half-way by a remnant of the massive old walls, called the Bargate. 'Above Bar'
was respectable and prim; 'Below Bar' grimmer and dingier
with, to the child's senses, a lowering, sinister feel. At the
waterside one came upon the Royal Pier, then gay with red
and green paint, little lights and the Isle of Wight ferries,
delightful small paddle-boats that chuffed down the Water

and across to Cowes. From the deck one saw thrilling things: the Calshot Supermarine Works (their record-breaking seaplane would become the Spitfire fighter), the vast and hideous sprawl of Netley Hospital – place of dread about which there were terrifying tales – and all down the water long-anchored rows of out-of-work freighters, abandoned save by a watchman. One would be reminded of the Depressional ways because comfy bourgeois Southampton, shopping at Tyrell and Green or Plummer Roddis, suddenly became harsh, and the working-class areas of Shirley or Woolston, Northam and the Six Dials, were not cosy.

This was not the industrial north, so vividly sickeningly brought to life by George Orwell. It was a small-scale version of London's East End, smelt of dirt, kippers and sewage but always with the disinfectant breath of the sea, would have been less starved and hopeless than Liverpool: here was the terminus of the transatlantic liners. Their trade was unaffected by hardship; this was indeed the heyday of Cunard and White Star. The rich came down by the boat-train, stopping at Southampton West but running on to the quayside. We did not see them, but we saw and knew the mighty army of the great liners' servants, attentively bowing, extremely underpaid. Flock upon flock of stewards and chambermaids, cooks and pantrymen – the victualling of a liner outdid any grand hotel in complexity and luxury. Another regiment of fitters and armourers, mechanics and greasers cleaned and repaired and maintained the fabric of these leviathans, which would sit outside and whimper (we knew the voice of every siren) for the flock of tugs to nurse them to their berths and tuck them in, while another was towed out, New York bound.

I do not count, here, – we didn't, under the spell of our own sovereignty – the ships of other nations; of the French Line, of Hamburg-Amerika or the stately Dutch ladies out of Rotterdam. They came to the Solent, and a tender brought out the passengers who so oddly preferred them. 'Ours' were lordly *Aquitania* and graceful *Berengaria*, splendid *Majestic* and *Olympic*. It is possible that White Star, always a bit mega-lo, was less well managed; succumbed at last to the ever so slightly second-rate Cunarders. We thought *Queen Mary* an awkward great cow when she came, and promptly stuck on the mud off Cowes. *Normandie* made a mighty dint in our vanity. But 'ours' were things schoolboys thought much of; 'world's biggest' dry- or floating-dock – in which last I saw *Majestic* from a small boat high above my head, frightening me out of an eight-year-old's fragile wits.

I had not heard of George Orwell. It is possible that Walter dipped into the Left Book Club – I can recall him infected by the Social Credit ideas. Why, apart from the dottiness and bad material judgment (both so familiar to me), should he buy and live in the little Ampthill Road house? Dingy little street opening on Foundry Lane, a hand's breadth from the dockland. Quite soon he would over-correct, into an appalling bourgeois villa named (one could not do better) 'Montreux', Midanbury Lane. Was Ampthill Road his 'time among the tramps', a half-hearted brush with Socialism and the poor? I recall little, but at this age impressions will surface many years later. Thus, for Walter had entries into this world, the sharpest memory is material … of standing on the deck of *Homeric* – she was due I was told to be broken up. I looked down, feeling vertigo and fear, into her tremendous engine-room.

Efforts were made, here I think on Nancy's side, to find children with whom to play, among the 'decent poor': it must have been seen that I was over-solitary, a shrinker. How else should I know the smell of Shirley houses; oil-cloth, tea, bread and marge? Why are names fixed in my memory? Pat Simmonds, Danny Baber? Nancy had also friends of higher-class style: how else would the names of two brothers (too old and too grand to play with a ragamuf-fin) come to mind? The elder was Humphrey, the younger Harley. I seem to have been a little Oliver Twist, with my posh accent and no notion how the poor play. I know only that Mrs Baber (Nancy loved her and that must go to the credit of both these honest women) was a hairdresser, told my poor mother that I was too old for lace collars and Fauntleroy ringlets, and cut my hair.

I liked and respected Pat and Danny. We could not be friends; the gap was too wide. But I was repaid richly for effort, some years later in the army. ('Who wants to be an officer? Fuck that.') A Barnsley boy taught me how to soldier. A south Wales boy taught me how to swing a shovel. 'Mate, you stupid. All your energy to waste, see?' Right: digging here the garden, in Grandfontaine, I remembered. During my Army service, many times, officers (little twits) spoke silly words. But my worker, north of England mates, so strangely clear-sighted, for they had been born in the back-to-backs, never – not for a single instant – let me down. I have some, maybe damned feeble socialist blood, but it runs deep, which Walter's didn't. Purely sentimental: no doubt: in Ampthill Road we buttered our bread. But something: please, let it be put to my credit.

'Montreux' was a house typical of its time and style, with a grandiose bay window at one corner, prolonged above into a turret. There was a large garden, with a greenhouse and a tennis court. This is mentioned because the fence to the roadway was covered in a thickish shrubbery of laurel, and here I hid for one entire day rather than go to school, frightened at every footstep but undetected; I imagine because I was often absent through illness and nobody bothered to enquire. It was a bad school – cheap, coarse, given to bullying; I had been persecuted by a gang which made horrid threats. I should think I was lucky that it did not rain. This was also the kind of school where children with no talent for arithmetic or gymnastics were jeered at and made to feel less than the worm.

At this time I became aware of the world and its divisions of opinion, known as politics. I have spoken of Nancy's early days as a Communist true-believer. Many friends from this time came often and stayed a few days. Discussion ran warm over the Spanish War; a good few former admirers were setting sail for the International Brigade. Alas, since poor Nancy had become so rabidly Catholic, all her sympathies, strongly (loudly) held, were Franco-colour. Never mind about Fascism; your damned Republicans go about raping nuns. I notice – sadly – that whatever I have said about childhood lacks humour, but here's a chance to put things right. Amid her already vast collection of Roman collars was a gang of earnest young Italian Fathers to whom she was Egeria. I think she was supposed to be teaching them English; my further guess is that *il Duce*, known for grandiose ambitions, had an eye upon English colonies in Northern Africa. Possibly these young men had to learn English in order to help in spreading the Faith among the infidel: I should like to have consulted the Duke of Pirajno, civilized and witty witness to those ludicrous goings-on.

Never mind, here is Nancy holding aloft the Cross and shouting hard, and perhaps half a dozen young poet intellectuals who had all been in love with her, unable to believe their ears. Tragedy needs these farcical interludes: stiff and solemn Cambridge boys practising their Spanish, while Nancy's tendency to talk French when excited had become newly enriched with kitchen-Italian. Yes it is funny but we didn't think so at the time. Perhaps Guadalajara put a stop to a little of the ecclesiastical enthusiasms. By the ending amid so much suffering of this war everyone was worrying about the next, she had made herself ill, and the new Irish mania was on the way to drive out doubts about the saintliness of Franco.

It was in 1935 that the family came to live in Bitterne Manor House, of which I have already written; I could not write more without falling into a juicy self-indulgence. Four years, until August 1939. Chequered years, with many sunbursts of great happiness. Reading enormously, playing strenuously, nearly always in solitude; Pat and Danny still appeared now and then but faded away. Two years (the only ones I have, alas) at a school where one learned something: I could find comedy too in a Jesuit headmaster of blessed eccentricity who used to smack our bare bottoms; the extraordinary thing is that nobody seems to have found this in the least abnormal or even worthy of comment.

Spitfires appeared in the innocent Hampshire sky, sandbags around the Civic Centre, and after Munich we were given gas masks. But Bitterne Manor House appeared secure, a haven which would always be there. When a child of twelve (young for the age, being over-sheltered) was suddenly snatched away, yes, I do think that this was a highly traumatic business. At the time I felt amputated, and looking now at a battered human being I am quite unsurprised.

Irritating since at best a slipshod usage is the habit of speaking about the past in terms of decades; journalists who weren't even born then saying airily that the 1970s – or whenever – were a time of this or that. The two sections, of childhood and adolescence, in my own past do fit neatly into these terms of reference. The 1930s were the English childhood of a little boy unsure of nearly everything and trying hard to belong: to a social class which in the depression years had lost most of the familiar landmarks; to a comfortable Englishness still settled and orderly, along this south coast still green and largely rural, where people had scarcely heard of the misery of the north, so close and so far. My father took me with him, putting our bicycles on a little puffing train, getting out in Sway or Brockenhurst to explore the New Forest: with Nancy our green Hants & Dorset buses took us to Winchester or Salisbury: we went down the water to the island, or the busy clattery Southern-electric to Portsmouth. A cosy, tight, delightful little world. London was a place of magic, of enormous unsuspected treats; and occasionally of the grim shadow of St Thomas's Hospital. There were times of acute pain, illness, exhaustion; more of the suffering a child does not understand, the not knowing where a blow will fall nor why, the lack of bearings, the search for sea-marks one had thought constant.

All this vanished overnight. A well-known story often told, that the blitz of the Luftwaffe in 1940 hit the south-coast ports with a sudden ferocity. Portsmouth, Plymouth – the naval bases – and Southampton among the hardest hurt. Bitterne Manor House itself (island of ancient privilege and splendour nestled in the curve of the river) was brought to the ground in ruins, but the English child had a year before been cut off with a snip of the scissors; no longer existed; had to create a new life from scratch. Everything known and trusted – home, school, comrades, country, and his father – dead in London, the long-threatened heart conquered.

Speaking of Nancy I found much to say of Ireland; speaking of a child of twelve growing into adolescence (the war would be virtually at an end and England changed out of a boy's recognition before he came as he thought 'home' and found a heap of ashes) I have nothing to say at all; like Bartleby the Scrivenor I prefer not to. I learned to love the long, amazingly still, night-time walks through beautiful Dublin. A boy's love affair of dizzying violence created a havoc, and ten years later scars still red and raw. Much more; the forties brought a great deal more pain and few enough of those moments of magical happiness which the memory later will cuddle, cherish, magnify into lost splendours. The 1940s began with the coal-smoke and fish smell of Euston station; ended with the same. In between came also the army time, really quite useless and of great boredom, as has often been said; I still maintain that for the boy I was, the experience had some real value). The 1940s ended with our young man back in France, another world that had suffered and seen mighty changes. But for the French the instinct to conserve is so strong, and to cling to the old ways however threadbare, that here I found more that seemed familiar and reassuring than I had in the England that had appeared distorted and as though surfaced after a long submersion, where even well-known landmarks seemed blurred, weed-hung. Did London smell the same? Yes, sometimes. But Paris, a city scarcely known in childhood, now gave instant welcome. The boy, for I was certainly not a man, had few holdfasts, resources, guide-lines; acquired giddily enough notions of a path to travel, a living to earn, and lessons to learn for this boy, the 1940s ended in hotel kitchens, having the nonsense kicked out of him. Looking back, the choice was not absurd.

I am not going to write here about 'my kitchens'. I did so in *The Kitchen Book*; *cela suffit*, and more would be boring. The classic witness to this world is Ludwig Bemelmans, a marvellous writer if sometimes sentimental in a false, coyly sugary manner when pot-boiling for tourist magazines. An incomparable draughtsman, he was a good painter, rather like Daumier a splendid caricaturist, and his cooks and waiters, drawn often on the backs of menus, are witty, loving and true; have poetry and pathos. This is what they were like. I so attest. An astonishing gift. These drawings too are gloriously funny.

It needs saying because George Orwell, a very good writer, in *Down and Out* wrote a weirdly bad book. His fierce bristling Englishness gets in the way of his honest eye; much that he sees was real but distorted by anger. It is sad how few Englishmen can write about France without this passion of hatred. Even the denunciations belong to the century before, will ring true in that context.

There were many vile survivals, and I have known them. The service areas in grand hotels were abominable; the dark unhygienic tunnels are not much exaggerated and working conditions dreadfully harsh. A cook though could always find better, for it is true that cooks were the aristocracy of the below stairs and a good cook was greatly prized. We were ill-paid, the hours were long and the kitchens at the twice-daily *coup de feu* were infernos. We were skilled craftsmen, and we took a great pride in our work. I do not hesitate to say that I was happy. If a place was really bad one could and did walk out. I would also have to say that the worst I have seen were not in France ...

Temperament has a lot to do with this. Like many disorganized and self-indulgent persons incapable of self-discipline, I liked to find myself under orders. Discipline in the big kitchens where the brigade counted up to forty cooks was of military severity: it had to be. An order was obeyed instantly and on the run, and was not questioned. The *fainéant* was shown the door within the hour. In this respect, it is true to say that the atmosphere was of nineteenth-century character, betimes still Nelsonian, and also that of Private Mulvaney, full of tall stories – and many of them true. Of my ten years as a cook five were spent in this antique and often terrible world. We found much to laugh at, and over an off-duty beer the day's campaign was recalled, discussed, relished; I will repeat, enjoyed. It is a constant truth that old men forget, and that I remember, with advantage, the deeds of those days.

Something of these essences persisted for years here in this house. In sleep I am again at the piano alerted by the formal hieratic cry, as from the muezzin, of *Ca marche, pour deux couverts* – so that I will sit up for a moment, take a drink of water. When I cook, and what I now do no longer merits the use of the word, I take a knife from the drawer. A cook's knives (some ten or twelve) tell another a great deal about his status, skills and experience. Their quality – the best are very dear – the wear they show, for they must be ground now and then. Some cooks carry about beloved old slivers of steel no longer usable which they cannot bear to throw away. The writer has no symbol of his craft. He may use thirty fresh-sharpened pencils, like Georges Simenon, and today he has probably a computer keyboard like any businessman, but a cook's quality depends now, as ever, upon his knives (which no one else may use). When, in 1961, I left my last kitchen I made a formal goodbye for by then I had published two books and was writing the third. I gave away most of my knives to colleagues; kept two. Mark Grandfontaine on the map: 'crossed swords'.

3

Interlude: a Handful of Field Flowers

O VER THIRTY YEARS we have not done much to the house, which had character enough of its own. At the beginning the builder, the plumber, the electrician, the carpenter, the central-heating man. We were ambitious enough to want comforts. These installations are now old; it is as though they've always been. One would wish now to modernize, to shake everything up and renew. Others will undertake the job.

I was the painter; nothing had been done in fifty years, and people who had lived here did not think in terms of 'taste'. Coming out for the weekend we brought – as everyone does – a piece of country furniture, some curtains, rolls of wallpaper, all now shabby, dilapidated or even worn out. As the children grew up they contributed – all of us working together changed the tiles of the roof. When the time came to shake free of Strasbourg many things were dumped here, since here one always found space. Attic and cellar filled as they always do with the junk one has no use for but is unwilling to throw away. And among all this, books. It is well known that throwing them away is fatal but one still does, by the armful: even in a house like this, hell, no space for all this junk. The boys have put up shelving of the cheapest wood and the most summary fit up in every room. Sixpence the kilo I suppose – fella in Hay-on-Wye. French rag-and-bone man probably would refuse to touch it at all; or would try to stick me with the cartage.

For everyone who likes books – I suppose I should say 'can't resist' since the act is compulsive – picks up some oddities, but also plenty of dreadful dogs. I am old enough (we are still quite numerous) to remember the invention of paperbacks in the mid-1930s; Allen Lane's extraordinary stroke of genius.

They cost sixpence, had a flexible but quite sturdy cover and even a paper dust-jacket; the early ones are now all collectors' items. A great many publishers said openly that it would never work – Lane must be off his nut – and quite a few refused to sell paperback rights in their own books, preferring to trust their own cheap editions, a well-tried system. Many of those were cheap in every sense, on bad paper, poorly printed and bound, inclined to disintegrate with wear. There was also Tauchnitz but these could only be sold outside the country.

There were also, selling for about a shilling and a marvellous buy, pocket-size editions, cloth-bound and thus genuine hardbacks, furthermore well printed on good paper, from firms like Nelson. The drawback, if that is the word, was that these were 'classics' (meaning roughly that the copyright had expired). I wish to make a note here of a personal sort. I have still a dozen of the Macmillan pocket editions of Kipling, quite flimsy but most attractively bound in a thin scarlet leather, gold-stamped and really beautiful productions. These have fallen to shreds but are treasured for having been bought by Nancy with a young girl's pocket-money.

The 'real paperbacks', even when much handled, resisted well. The bindings had been properly sewn and the lay out given decent margins. When opened they stayed open. Lane's insistence upon high standards paid off. In wartime the paper was poor quality but – surely up to 1950 and even perhaps beyond – they were stubbornly maintained to honest standards. Thereafter it was all downhill and progressive cost-cutting took its toll; the thin cramped look, the quart stuffed in a pint pot – and much worse was to come when someone who had certainly never read a book attempted the vile economy of gluing the pages; a sinister calamity.

None of this stops the book-slave, whose need of print is such that he reads the 'notice for usage' wrapped round medicine bottles, and other peoples' newspapers upside-down, which leads to startling conclusions. He'd buy anything rather than leave empty-handed. Even the very bad will bitterly contest efforts to throw them away. Shelves fill with information one might one day want, and even fiction which might prove worthy if read in the right frame of mind. There is luckily a large category of good bad-books, to distinguish from the bad good-book, which takes itself very seriously. The good-bads are a happier lot and one very often needs them when lonely, ill or just sad; they will lift the heart and enliven the imagination. There are many famous ones (like James Bond, or from a generation before the Scarlet Pimpernel). My example would be on many lists: John Buchan indeed is still spoken of in awestruck tones; often still cited by publishers on jackets (they haven't, as a rule, read a book in years, having long learned to 'do without').

He had many good qualities: a well paced story in simple classical prose; a sense of landscape and nature, close to earth and near the sky; love and understanding of flower and bird. It does not do to say that he was a fearful old fascist, to mutter at the anti-Semitism, the snobbery and condescensions: his was the empire-building world, South Africa for the white man. It was the age of Rhodes and Milner and appalling Baden-Powell; he couldn't help it. Risible, rather than merely laughable, is the queenie coyness; Sandy looks like a girl while heroines are praised for looking like boys . . . or that Hannay speaks 'perfect German' while the Honourable Arbuthnot is both a Turkish gypsy and a South American gangster who can take in the genuine article. We are rescued from both Dornford Yates and Bulldog Drummond by a distinction of mind: Buchan really could read Latin and Greek and it isn't all ignoble. The silliness must not swamp us: I am trying to say that we must not condescend. A really good writer – both Dickens and Kipling come at once to my own mind – must be read in his, and our, wholeness. We were fascinated and delighted in our green years, in which we also cultivated burning scorn, and the most slashing condemnations came so readily, so easily. One must come back to the ripeness of a great writer when we too are ripe. Even a Buchan bears fruit in his later years. That should give hope to writers who had talent, but did not develop, perhaps because they were constantly drunk or were wounded, often fatally, by bad women. Few now have the patience to wait for ripeness: this is green banana world.

Indeed a Buchan character, after some preposterous derring-do on an island, says 'I'm coming back here to make my soul ... You know well enough what I mean. The Norlands are a spiritual place which you won't find on any map.' What? 'Make his soul'; what does he mean by that? Clearly enough it is what I have been fishing for these many years in this poor little corner; a vague and woolly expression. They ought to do better, having been brought up on the Book of Common Prayer, where the phrasing of quite commonplace ideas is in the noblest language.

After the deaths of children and grandchildren, a great man of the fifteenth century (when life was extremely cheap) while looking round his palace was heard to say 'Too large a house now for so small a family'. A phrase of mine also when praying, in gratitude that my own children are so near. Cosimo de' Medici spent long hours in silence, we are told. (Christopher Hibbert's book is another of my 'field flowers'.) Why so much time alone without speaking, his wife wanted to know. 'When we are going away you spend a fortnight preparing for the move. Since I have soon to go from this life to another, don't you understand how much I have to think about?' My own wife asked with a slight irritation why I sit with my eyes shut. I wish I had thought of Cosimo's answer, which was 'To get them used to it'.

Further along, busy now with Lorenzo the Magnificent, his wife dies. Clarice Orsini was Roman, a prim woman rather full of her own aristocratic family. She detested Florence – vulgar crowd – never felt at home there. Understood nothing about art or architecture, loathed politics, couldn't abide his noisy splendid world. They had very little to say to each other. When away, as he mostly is, he writes kind, gentle, empty letters, about the weather and not catching cold. He had plenty of mistresses – gay and elegant, funny and charming – and would have more. He is shattered by her death; the hole made can never be repaired. One cannot pretend to understand 'marriage'. My own is the greatest treasure I have; I don't in the least understand it.

Another flower: Dickens at the end of his extraordinary writing life (the last pages of his last finished book) asks about Lizzie's marriage to Eugene; can it possibly work? (Feeble little Twemlow gives a noble answer; no one else has courage, dignity, or generosity.) Two points come to mind. One of course is that Dickens was himself the worst possible husband: the other is that he could never write a young and thus marriageable female character. In this same book Bella Wilfer, a spirited, delightful, funny girl, disintegrates before our eyes into an abject sentimental doll.

Lizzie Hexam is the best by far. The – unsentimentally humble – daughter of the Bird of Prey is never a mawk; even rescuing Eugene from death she is real (and Eugene never progresses from the languid cigar-smoking propounder of Oscar Wilde witticisms). It takes the dolls' dressmaker to bring them together. I prefer to believe that Jenny Wren (I agree with Eugene that one can quickly become wearied of her) is a metaphysical invention sent by the Daimon, rather than merely another of Dickens' wonderful grotesques. It is certain that this is the case with Miss Flite: over the next world the Court of Chancery will have no power. I have little doubt about Mr F's aunt, who is 'sent' for a stronger purpose than merely to torment that sad drink of water Arther Clennam. I am less clear about Miss Havisham, but she too is 'sent' to scourge both Pip and Estella to the bare bone before their release. That Dickens knew nothing about marriage is a truism: as Orwell remarks, his 'resolutions' are nothing but to procreate *ad infinitum* while eating interminable gigantic meals. Did he begin to glimpse something of the truth, before the end?

Neither of the supreme masters – Stendhal and Flaubert – will have any truck with anything of the sort. (I do not pretend to any understanding or appreciation of the Russian masters.) '*On est tout seul, ma poule*'; a mistress can be loved with rare intensity but the 'artist' cannot admit her to the fortress that at all cost he must keep intact. The artist who chooses, aware of his deep-seated psychological inadequacy, to give himself to his chosen wife, lays up for himself the bitterest pains with the most intense of joys. (I wished to write *the* biography of Kipling but the distinguished publishers in both London and New York had no stomach for it: they were right, of course.) One cannot write about an artist's marriage. One cannot know; one cannot apprehend, and neither an emotional nor intellectual point of departure can give us any clue whatever to what – say – Fanny Osborne meant to Robert Louis Stevenson.

Leonora's cry 'I am his wife' is enough. After that, there is no more to say.

4

Garden Days, Gaudy Nights

THE VILLAGE, which is many things, and to more people, and is also this house, is also the garden: one must prepare for something rich and strange, and dotty.

The village, in I suppose a geological sense, since it is the soil and stones, the air and water, belongs to the valley and is held in common. An accident of property secured some three acres of mountain meadow and a piece of valley-bottom to the house. But that is quite a vague concept, since this ground called mine is split in half by the roadway up to the Minières, and the road is a public place over which I have no mastery. The bottomland is itself bisected by the brook, which belongs to the national ministry called *Les Eaux et Forêts*. These legal constraints are not very clearly defined but encroach upon me: I have sometimes planned things and found myself forbidden to execute the project. On this north side of the house my will is subject to the Commune, and supposedly the communal good. I cannot complain of that. There are other public authorities, also with a say in matters. On 'my land' are four antique wooden poles which support electricity cables. I have had passages with the local engineer of *Electricité de France*, a pleasant and kind-hearted man. We came to an amiable compromise over the trees which he said – quite rightly – made for dangers and difficulties to his service. To my suggestion that in the modern world these cables are buried underground he smiled. France is large, and the rural areas are backward and impoverished. I should I think be grateful that he has not – as yet – proposed to implant metal pylons, which would be larger and a much greater eyesore.

Thus – to be brief, this northern terrain bristles with ditch and caltrop, mantraps and spring guns. I do well at present to leave it alone. On the steep slope beyond the brook I have some twenty trees of my own planting. Some have stood thirty years and approach adult life. A few were mistakes and have had to be cut. A few are beautiful. All are shapely bar one which I cannot bear to extinguish and one broken by storm wind. All are loved.

It is a pity, all this. On both sides of the brook is (as one would expect) deep and fertile ground. Here indeed the former owners had a sketch of kitchen garden. Within the narrow confines of the village, and the harsh upland climate, there is no room for agriculture. But horticulture certainly. The children will decide upon this point.

The stony, ungrateful, steep meadow remained, south of the house and contiguous with the buildings, climbing to the surrounding forest. When we first came to the village this still carried signs of the historic way of life here; it was an integral part of the tiny hill farm. It had long been cleared of tree-stumps and the invasive brambly undergrowth. It was a true meadow, scythed for hay and fertilized by sheep. For the road was an old transhumance way from the Alsace lowlands to the high summer pasturage, and flocks had been rested here overnight. To see this though as garden required an effort of imagination which took ten years to make. The first word that comes would have to be 'comic'. Spoken quite kindly; only the children called me loony to my face. Nowadays there is admiration, and the boys silenced by themselves having to do whatever takes muscular effort; something I've run short of. I can be forgiven since all the early stages were my single-handed work. Initial disbelief has given way to respect. The slope is too steep for mechanized equipment, and all was done by hand.

This mountain flank has three basic constituents. One is the topsoil, of fine quality but thin; there is never enough of it. To collect, as greedily as an usurer weighing coins. Little buckets of the treasure stood about, ready to be inserted into niches. Two was the subsoil, vile stuff of a nasty ochre colour due to the iron content of the hill (all around us are the former shafts and workings of the mines). This was conveyed in a barrow and wheeled off to be used as fill elsewhere. Three, the stones: a great many, but a happy (geological?) accident had broken most to a size one could manhandle. I enjoyed these: it was exciting to uncover one, to scrape it free hoping that it would be the right shape – to crowbar it out and go on digging until it could be heaved and wiggled into position as a fine new piece of drystone-walling; an art painfully learned: most of mine tumbled down and some-times twice until time, patience and crushed fingernails taught the trick of this ancient craft. A stone too big to shift (mercifully few) meant rethinking the design of the terracing, which followed some eccentric courses. Smaller stones are inserted to bed and stabilize the bigger, to complete intervals and level fronts. Sticking-out bits became footholds as one got higher. One of these walls, in the deep central bay, reached a height of nearly four metres. Of course these are not vertical; they are canted inward and bedded into the hill.

A hillside is not regular; there are both hummocks and hollows. Flatter bits where progress was faster, and the odd patch naturally so steep that it was better left untouched; the tough mat of plant roots will be more stable than any wall-ing. This labour, of some fifteen years, meant that the lower courses were thickly planted, with growth well established, which I was still carving and chiselling on the height. The whole goes up now, at an angle steep enough when seen from our windows, to a level clear of the house's roof-tree; to look down from the top can induce vertigo.

Physical satisfactions, excitements; hardly illegitimate and perfectly tolerable in those like myself to whom the word 'sport' has to have the prefix 'spectator' attached: if I kick a football it will go backwards. Not a bad word, 'sport'; the simplest definition would include the noun/verb 'play' – a basic human activity necessary to support life, as much as eating or sleeping. Comes from 'disport' and meant to amuse oneself. Gardening I should think falls under this heading.

More than that though; gardeners get very serious indeed. Sports are serious. They have to obey elaborately codified sets of rules and people come to blows about them. Hmm, go back a bit; *ludere*, 'to play' and 'ludic' (says the dictionary) is spontaneous play: spontaneous applies to gardens a good deal, right enough. (The children's game of Ludo has also led to blows; that's almost a rule.) Could one talk about an art? A moment ago I was talking about carving and chiselling, up above the house roof, which sounds like Mount Rushmore, a singularly unludic kind of sculpture. One must not be pompous in gardens.

The idea of art goes back a long way. Oriental carpets, which may not portray the human likeness – that would be to insult God – are full of gardens. A divine attribute; we know about the Garden of Eden (or as Marlene Dietrich was to learn, the desert is the Garden of Allah). Throughout history gardeners have been honoured, and deservedly – 'Abdolonymus was a gardener and for his virtue made King of Syria.' Come to that, the resurrected Christ was thought to be a gardener and nobody found this in the least odd.

I am tumbling into metaphysics with horrid speed. Avoiding the human likeness a tree is the greatest beauty, a flowering plant the greatest miracle. The mathematician I suppose will disagree, but to this beautiful crystalline world I have no key. 'God made the integers'; a mighty gift but not to me. The exact is divine. The inexact, since no leaf is the perfect likeness of the other, no less so. Perhaps our duality, our separateness and togetherness, our never-wholeness, is here shown us. What is given us, that we have to work with. The gift of the gardener is as great as any that we know of. I do not have it.

Gardens are noticeably a blessing shared largely among the English. That fortunate island has much to be grateful for. Perhaps it would be found (but all such calculations can only estimate material benefits) that this lump of the world's land surface has been strangely blessed. Were it calculable we might also find a peculiar balance of affairs. Being myself English I might say that we appear to be the worlds's most boastful and self-satisfied of folk, but that . . .

The English aim for spontaneity in gardens. Ludic, distinctly – now and then ludicrous. A French garden is a highly formal concept, an extension of architecture, of straight lines and perspectives: one could easily get led astray here into a long discussion about art. One might pause for a second to wonder whether Italy is not the most openly and evidently blessed of all the comical pieces that make up the European jigsaw, since here the sense of design – so strong – happily balances the classical and the romantic in the garden. Imagination we have (fair bulging with it), but the English design is a potato. We are good at importing. We mustn't complain since nowhere else is there such a genius for poetry. My own garden – ludicrous would be the first word to come to mind – perhaps compensates me. There is more poet here than peasant.

One learns much about design – even the word is Italian – by looking at trees; there are stupid-looking trees but not many. Some of the best are forbidden us by climate: olives won't grow in the north. Keen explorers, tremendous acquirers, the English have been the most avid of plant collectors, but the word does them less than justice; there is a strong sense of grabbing before anyone else gets there but also, and one might think stronger, is the scientific interest, a passion for knowledge, a fierce curiosity – yes and a delight too in beauty: one can find it all in Mr Pepys (with much light shed upon the early days of The Royal Society). This I think is reflected in the collections of commercial plant nurseries and small gardens as well as huge famous ones. Somewhere there a breath of pollen dust blew off and a trace stuck to me.

Years passed before I planted anything. The mechanical excavator rushed about robot-like puffing and sparking – there seemed always to be another large stone, a couple more tipper-loads of that nasty subsoil. At the start, it is true I planted some twenty trees to 'give the eye something to look at' and some of these, now near adult status, are there still, an abiding joy. For years also, an obsession with water ate up available energies. The brook was diverted into a large pond, for which visions of water-lilies and irises danced like sugar-plums in my head: since this water flows out of the old mines and has a high iron content nothing will live in it. While on the south terrace an immovably big rock was of a shape and rhythm that insisted upon the making of a cascade, with a fountain above. Ferns grow in the rockface ... I clung for twenty years to this project but went about it with so amateurish and unskilful a hand that it never worked properly, and when at last I resolved to have it done professionally the expense had become prohibitive: I have never quite forgiven myself for being daunted, and it remains my immense failure: there have been so many more. By then I was planting things, and wondering why so few seemed to thrive.

A state of affairs which never did get cleared up. Knowledgeable people look at a clump of (common-or-garden) iris which year after year affords two blooms where there should be twenty; fall silent. The soil is right, the plants are healthy, the exposure good. Maleficent influence somewhere and it can only be me. They can't even say, sighing rather as when all the pinks died, 'Dianthus need chalk' – which everyone knew but me. Nor can I take credit for the obvious; the nice thing about azaleas is that they do bloom here and so does anything which likes acid soil, not much sun (and plenty of snow), has a woody bushy habit, and has not objected to being moved a few times until we got the positioning right.

Typically, in the wilds of stolid Somerset was found an Englishman with a passion for maples so avid that he's forever going to Japan and finding more. I can't think why this had not occurred to us earlier; Japanese painting is all of landscapes like our own. Narrow valleys, defiles steep-sided, outcrops of reddish sandstone. Their conifers are ours and so are the deciduous sorts. The grasses – here is our fluid mountain grass, needle-fine and rain-loving. The English passion for lawns has no place there nor here; there is nowhere to play croquet.

Maples are elegant, flexible, astonishingly varied. Their slightly artificial aesthetic look (as though cut out with sharp scissors by many clever patient hands) is also humble. No matter how odd or awkward my little nooks there is an unassuming charmer whose style and port will be right; upright and even stiff; bendingly meltingly feminine. They will even obey human proportions and keep to head-height, arms' breadth. Whereas our northern slope, a dreadful wilderness of weed but with a finely distanced perspective, has been ennobled by the tall and arrogant Vermont sorts whose autumnal colours are better known than their delicate spring growth.

But what is it all for? A passage of self-indulgence tipping over into self-congratulation. I have drawn the outline of a picture; now, like a child with coloured pencils, I start filling in the intervals. The child enjoys this occupation, and it is good training in co-ordination of the hand and the eye, in patience, in learning to make neat work, keeping the paper clean. But what adult purpose does this garden serve? Like most of my activities it is laughable.

An eccentric – factors are perceivable from birth giving me an eccentric bent – I can point to this garden as amiably dotty, a typical example of all that I do. It is imaginative; it is original and even creative. Beauty is there; it is a piece of art. Self-defeating to be sure. The concept was ridiculous; nobody could make a garden under these conditions, and it would occur to nobody else to try. Even short-term, within the bounds of my life, it is absurd since already I cannot provide the effort needed to maintain it. The boundary set, a widish

arc or crescent cut into the broader, deeper stretch of meadow, was planted with a hedge, the varied 'paradise' hedge the
English like, of flowering bushes mixed with different shades
and textures of evergreen yew, box or thuya. Such things
unless clipped severely and quite frequently will sprawl and
become a tangle, with enormous weeds flourishing (happy,
sheltered and protected) in the centre of ungainly foliage. I
have neither the strength nor the courage to put a stop to
this. There are things which have got too big and now deprive others of light. Quite so, every garden is like this. If at
all properly planned, and if these corrections are made, the
garden would be a legacy, something for generations to
come. This, the moment my hand is no longer stretched over
it, will be within a year again the rankest grass, the coarsest
weed.

Perhaps a professional gardener, called in for consultation,
will find a few plants (smallish, compact and of course expensive) worth transplanting; the rest will be 'Past saving
I'm afraid'. Asked whether anything can be done with the
terrain it would be 'Too steep and too much bloody bracken'.
One with Nineveh-and Tyre? A handful of dead leaves. I feel
no alarm; what of our activities knows a different fate? Does
one burn to be a bleak little mention in the *Dictionary of
National Biography*? It will be found that this all blows away
as dust. The author of *Gone with the Wind* – who achieved as
much immortality as anyone – will have been greatly delighted to have found that title which was even better than
she knew.

Does some metaphysical trace persist? A sediment. This is
the exact contrary of accepted wisdom. Heavy metals persist
in soil or water, and some particularly nasty chemicals are so
long-lived, as well as so dangerous, that we bury them in
concrete and shove them down the salt-mine. We would wish
to hear no more of them but they won't go away.

What, meanwhile, persists in the Chinese poet?

Li Po also died drunk.
He tried to recapture
The Moon in the Yellow River.

And is now one with a few million peasants: laconic footnote
saying 'Displaced by government engineering works upon
said river; died of flood, famine or epidemic illness. Statistics
unavailable as to who, where or how many'. Didn't Christ say
something about not a sparrow shall fall? Not that this
would be much consolation to the peasant, who accepted his
lot. Complaints to the Préfecture won't advance you much.
We have been told that ancestors are very important to these
peoples who, even when very humble, cherished their tombs,
made of them shrines with plants, flowers, some specially
beautiful object, perhaps a small sacred tree; came here to
pray. Our Western gardens after all are nothing much. If a
temple to anything at all, then to vanity and self-glorification.
'My' roses. It can be very odd how that little dusting (I called
it a sediment) of the spirit can still persist around these vulgar contraptions, but under God tree and flower belong only
to themselves.

The word 'dust' was deliberate because there is also a physical dust, of the bones of those who have gone before: any of
us may without knowing it have ingested a fragment of genius. The biologist has learned how to isolate morsels of gene,
to splice or implant. He dreams of producing a strong man,
mighty jumper or runner; a nauseating ambition but mercifully also laughable. The metaphysics of man which we call
the soul – even if he were to scrape together all the genetic
bits and pieces it still wouldn't be Schubert, it wouldn't be
Vermeer or John Donne. God can call to himself the bones of
the saints, but God knows how He does it. A garden embody-
ing the dust of all my ancestors – a rather fine idea. It would
need to be the whole world, wouldn't it? – literally the garden
of Allah. Never mind; even in the most humble garden one
can find a metaphysical space and meditate therein.

5

A Writer

WHAT GENES WENT TO THIS? My parents were book-lovers; like the millions more of their kind in the civilized world trained and brought up to love and respect this object, the fruit of thought and imagination; the skill and ingenuity of print and page and binding to culminate in a thing you can put in your pocket, to read Plato on a sailing-ship off Cape Horn or Proust in my bed at home. Indeed my mother herself tried her hand at writing; beyond her I have no idea of any ancestral skill or genetic affinity. A pace back I remarked that a metaphysical dust floats – settles? – informs our human activities. Genetics dictate. Environment plays a strong role here; a plant will grow and flourish in unlikely, quite unsuitable soil. A European ground nourished me; this air of Grandfontaine which I have tried feebly and inadequately to describe, I have been breathing these near-forty years. Why not poet or philosopher? My father had a bent for biology; was that a weaker or recessive gene? A prose fiction writer, a crime-novelist.

This needs some definition; I have spoken and written on the subject but it is so plunged in myth, surrounded by a fog of misconception and poor understanding, that now I must try to pull thinking together into a paragraph or so.

Strictly speaking crime is the pathology of human behaviour; a distortion growing into malignance and cancer is the cellular equivalent. Since the human being acts every imaginable fantasy, is a stranger to no errant or aberrant behaviour, we can accept a looser definition of crime. An action which growing from merely irresponsible impulse ends by causing irreparable damage. In the simplest expression physical – a killing, a mutilation, a rape. Obviously, an equally irreparable psychological damage can and does have small, sly, nigh-innocent beginnings. This is the fabric of prose fiction since the beginnings of time. With the rarest exceptions every story is a crime story. This is buried in the roots of psychiatry. Red Riding Hood is a physical crime; the Sleeping Beauty a psycho: both are lurid, commonplace, universal. Again with rare exceptions (Jane Austen doubtless the most familiar) all adult fiction is rooted in crime. The conventional summits of art in prose fiction develop the theme in a universal context.

This can be lurid, violently blood-spattered, as in Dickens or Dostoevsky, Stendhal or Melville. Or, just as often, silent, obliquely suggested, as it were secretive; Conrad uses both methods. Violence openly expressed carries the risk of vulgar melodrama, and will often be more effective when occulted; detached, ironic, blackly funny. All this is truism and to dwell on it invites banality. Shakespeare's audience liked its murders straight-up (a bucket of blood the hardest-worked stage property), but the killing of Duncan is immeasurably heightened by being unseen.

The crime need not even be physical: violence is as oppressive and as deadly when conceived and expressed in the mind of the sadist – the leverage of the strong character over the weaker. People can be driven to despair and death in the quietest undertone; it is none the less a murder when there are no knives handy. And to be sure, destruction may be orchestrated to appear as the work of the Fates – the Kindly Ones. Powell's splendid work, *A Dance to the Music of Time* seems no more than a gently-unrolling, richly comic tale of English society over a lengthy time-span. Pamela Widmerpool is given to abrupt violent movements, shocking but apparently trivial – being sick in the church font as a child, or while in the army slapping Stevens. It will take some time to understand the destruction and slaughter that follow in her wake: several deaths are put to her count, culminating in her own. The fearful woman in Ford's *The Good Soldier* is not more deadly.

Some of the very greatest achievements of prose fiction are not crime stories even when full of crimes and their consequences: I don't think we could accept either *A La Recherche du Temps Perdu* or *Ulysses* any more than *Don Quixote* or *Persuasion*. But these are, one can claim confidently, a special category. It is as though the individual vision, of extraordinary force and intensely personal, achieved thereby a wholeness, a universality of human experience in which good and evil have been judged, and we catch glimpses of a world beyond that unending battle; but such books are very rare. In the world to which we are born, from which only death frees us, it does not take long to lose our innocence. Throughout our lives, the baseness of our nature predominates. Evil wins, all along the line. But there is to us a spiritual nature, and good struggles to make itself known. Writing describes the conflict. The novelist makes use of talents given him, which he endeavours to put to good service; humour and imagination, irony and wit, accuracy of eye and ear; a sense of design to give shape to his little plot and project. But what will it be but a commentary on the moral problem, a note upon the theological enigma?

One man wrote a huge book upon a tremendous scale, Europe-wide, about tyranny and revolution, justice and liberty; love too and death; called it *War and Peace*. Another man wrote a book about exactly the same thing, whose physical setting is s few square metres of hillside on the shore of an Italian lake; called it *Piccolo Mundo Antico* – which sounds rather like Grandfontaine. The bigger is not on that account the better. Victor Hugo wrote a vast, lurid and magnificent description of the battle of Waterloo. Stendhal wrote about the same scene. Nothing happens; Fabrice gets his horse stolen. Everyone knows which is the better book and the greater art. Oh well, we all do what we can.

I began with no ideas at all except that I wanted to write; no – had to; it was an overwhelming necessity. I drew upon a few scraps of experience concerning a love affair with a married woman, which instinct told me was a crime, and thus a basis for crime writing. Various melodramatic doings were inserted into this story: a novel has to move along a rising line, and heightening devices are called for. A policeman came into it – this was another recent experience – making it, to my surprise, a detective story. Or so I was told.

I was like a man in the service of the Indian Geographical Survey, perhaps, tramping the foothills of the Himalaya, with an amateur interest in botany. He put some seeds in an envelope, wrote on the outside the place and date, added his name; enclosed a note saying 'Odd little thing but pretty; if it comes up it might be a nice surprise'; sent it off to Kew. He had just discovered the dwarf rhododendron...

My own funny little thing was received with enthusiasm and when published got ecstatic reviews. People said 'More' and obedient (I did not give myself the time to be bewildered and was incapable of thought) I turned out half a dozen. Ranging over the hills, small variations in soil or climate, altitude and exposure produced a series.

The metaphor is not bad. It happens that a plant is raised, copied, hybridized in nurseries all over the world. For the market it is tinkered with. Perhaps it can be made sturdier and longer flowering. Variations are found with bigger and brighter blooms, in other colours commercially more attractive. The original plant may prove capricious or be subject to mildew, and after a few years one would scarcely recognize it. I have seen it in many variations (selling tremendously for it proved popular) and often with amusement, sometimes with a shade of bitterness. There is no copyright in an idea, any more than in a plant; anyone can take it up and embellish it. I have met writers who were honest, saying openly 'Yes that was yours; I did nothing but copy it'. Others were slyer. Parasitism can even be unconscious; is it then a compliment? In any case the plagiarist is hard to pin down and one learns to disregard them. That odd scrapbag from which 'character' is shaped – is it even one's own? Who does it belong to? Courts of law much dislike being asked to decide the ownership of ideas. What matter? Move on to something else.

A series writer can make an excellent career for himself doing nothing but repeating his successful hit with a few superficial variations, and indeed this is the best way of protecting himself because this is what the public knows him for. Legitimate but boring. After a dozen of my own self-parodies (this is also called 'rounding' a character) I sought a ruthless remedy. Killing off the central figure 'isn't done' and Sherlock Holmes was forced back, if unconvincingly, from the Reichenbach Fall. Publishers were angry with me.

There was no more thought to this than there had been ten years before. The ground had got badly trampled; one moves higher up the mountain. In childhood I had a book with an illustration of

> Then felt I like some watcher of the skies
> When a new planet swims into his ken

– a sort of lonely shepherd perched upon a rock; in Greece perhaps? Mount Olympus? There were lots of stars. Romantic stuff. In fact the new planet much resembled the old one, acquiring also a variety of mannerisms, but of more technical skill, within a wider looser context, and I should hope of more capacity for thought; it seems to me that this offered much more scope. A pity that the buyers in the market-place never really agreed with me. The fault – dear Brutus – was in being too far ahead of the times in which we live.

I have always detested nationalism. Kipling's jelly-bellied flag-flapper, who thought that crude empire-building chauvinism would suit the idealist patriotism of a schoolboy audience, is still very much with us. He can be seen at sporting events, madly waving his Union Jack. The *tifosi*; the *Schlachtenbummler* – these ridiculous names are appropriate. The team's fans are ordinary people and one has no quarrel with them. The beer-drinkers who are looking for a good punch-up with the police don't bother me either since they haven't much fun and want some excitement; worrying the police and frightening shop-keepers are not serious crimes. They may be nasty but hooligans are preferable to going to war. While nationalists are forever on the verge of going to war: their aggressivity, today and no doubt tomorrow, provokes appalling catastrophes. In the old countries of western Europe, particularly those which have lost empires and still feel nostalgia for vanished grandeurs, one need not take it very seriously; a lot of gas about sovereignty; impassioned appeals for defiance of the bureaucrats and bankers whose chief offence was to be 'foreigners'. Nationalism in England, France or Spain is an antiquated sentiment, crystallized and as it were codified in the seventeenth century. In Germany or Italy, politically unified only a century ago, sentiment can be forgiven for running higher, and several countries further east have found their frontiers redefined yesterday so that national uproar is still immature and unstable.

Shortly after the last Great War, I was still young and full of ideals. The handful of statesmen who agreed upon the European Community knew that the realization would take two generations; they were slow, prudent and frightened of making mistakes. One effect, however, has come to fruit in my lifetime, and to us on the frontier, here in Grandfontaine, it is the most important of all. It is the impossibility of war, death, destruction, disruption, homelessness and bitter poverty, between France and Germany.

I have pretty good reasons for calling this part of the world my own. The physical section of the present book makes it clear that the frontiers of the Rhineland, established, attacked and bitterly disputed over since the beginnings of documented history, are political fictions which were made the pretext for blood-baths from Roman times to our own day. The Rhine and the Meuse (north of Liège called the Maas) have been crossed and recrossed almost without interruption by the peoples of Europe in arms: I know of no equivalent to this unending disaster. The creation of Belgium, due to Talleyrand whose lifelong work was peace between England and France, put indeed a stop to these incursions – as the independence of Holland has made an end of Spanish ambitions in the area. It took the work of the Treaty of Rome in our days to ensure that Germany would not again invade Northern France, and that France would never again dream of occupying Cologne. Charlemagne's old capital of Aachen would have been a good choice in which to house the Community, but Brussels fills the role well enough.

To the best of our knowledge the forebears of my wife and myself belong here, have lived and suffered here. Our taking up quarters in Strasbourg, at the southernmost point of this world, was not the accident it seemed at the time. (The French occupation of Amsterdam was brief and inglorious.) In this land of extreme violence, of burned wood and twisted metal soaked in European blood, the writer finds fertile source.

It is often said and with much truth that the energies of a writer are observable in his capture of a particular landscape. When – to cite a well-known example – Ian Fleming wrote about his beloved underwater world he wrote well; with a truth, simplicity, acuity unobservable in his advertising-agency pages. A better example is Raymond Chandler making the area between Los Angeles and Santa Monica his own. While to find something held in common with Kipling's Sussex, Hardy's Dorset, is a compliment to warm any writer's heart.

6

CASTANG'S CITY

REVIEWING A BOOK WITH THIS TITLE a fair-minded woman made the guess that 'it just had to be Toulouse'. She was mistaken but I was pleased; I had wanted it to be anywhere in France, for the central figure was still loose in my mind and footloose in background – I had not then defined either the man or his world.

The early books had been set in Holland. The personage of van der Valk was from the start an Amsterdammer: in no other town would he have learned a sharpness of wit and a sophistication of mind that were his. It was very improbable in fact that he should ever have chosen the police as profession; a familiar problem to all writers of this kind of book and probably the reason for the talented amateur sleuth, eccentric and often drunk, who can disregard police procedures and legal constraints, and generally manages to make the professionals look slow and stupid. This type of figure had been around a long time and become increasingly tedious. If any realism is sought – even a dab at the realities of social condition – crime and its consequences are the affairs of the police. Since the truth of all police work is trivial, squalid and hidebound by bureaucratic regulation and unending paperwork, the writer relies upon devices that would get a genuine police officer fired inside a week. Mr van der Valk was dotty, undisciplined, insubordinate – not very Dutch; was even given a French wife. It is not surprising that he soon began to ramble about, turning up oddities while on holiday – these ploys are common to this kind of book.

Years before, Simenon's Maigret had found solutions to these difficulties. He concerns himself very little with the hierarchy of the Quai des Orfèvres. He has a number of devoted dogsbodies for the tiresome details of investigation and verification; himself loiters about with his pipe, drinking a lot. His real concern is with the psychological realities, the behaviour of people caught and squeezed by human quandary. Indeed this fine writer became bored by the Maigret canon, wrote them as pot-boilers, and at his publisher's insistence. With fewer gifts I found myself the prisoner of conventions I could see little future for. Was it not possible to attempt something more original, and firstly less hemmed about by the needs of a public insatiable for more of the same?

Castang's character assembled itself, piece by piece and through several books; from a youngish man, full still of innocence and ignorance, until a retirement some little bit wiser and made slyer by experience, sceptical and occasionally cynical. He was – as I was myself – let loose in France, a wider scope for multifarious doings than the fairly constricted atmosphere of Holland. He was not and never could be French: one of my mistakes was in not making this clear at the start. How was it that this man, French in his sympathies and for long in loyalties, but seldom in feeling and less still in thinking, occupied positions of responsibility in the Police Judiciaire, sworn servants of the State, a place in which deeply-seated French prejudices, devotions and traditions are manifest?

As a young man, he felt French by inclination and training: his scepticism, his individuality and indiscipline were of a sophisticated Parisian sort, common enough in a cosmopolitan city. He was an illegitimate child, born anonymously in a Paris hospital; it is the right of a Frenchwoman to conceal her identity in childbirth. The baby is often abandoned, to become pupil of the nation. In fact he was brought up by an aunt, a small Paris shop-keeper. A householder, of some substance; such are deemed respectable citizens, and when she assumed the responsibilities of guardianship few questions were asked. She was tight-lipped about the child's mother,

and probably never knew who the father was. It only occurred to me later that around this time – towards the end of
the war – a good many English and American soldiers had
passing love affairs in Paris. It would have been quite likely
that he did not even know he had fathered a child. This
would explain the behaviour of the aunt, herself an unmar-
ried woman of strong character.

The evidence is simply that the child grew up with quite a
strict upbringing and a lot of love, but solitary and unaware
of being in obscure ways different. To be bright is a help. In
the formal, rather arid, rigid structure of French schools before the revolution of 1968 (the Education ministry used to
be called Public Instruction) there was room for the gifted
child who accepted hard work, much punishment and occasional praise, and harsh conditions. Many of the teachers
were talented and devoted men. (There were few women
then in this world.) Such a child once noticed would pass
quite easily the severe formal examinations of entry to the
lyceum, the baccalaureate, and a university diploma. The boy
was also street-sharp and used his eyes and ears.

There is a further point which would have a good deal of
importance in Castang's future. The little shop of Ma Tante
dealt in artists' materials; paper and canvas, crayons and
colours. From an early age the child was accustomed to seeing painters, hearing them talk, knowing their jokes and
complaints, their realities, for most were poor and scraped a
chancy living, and their visions. This introduction to the cultural imagination and a world in which the arts were of
meaning and importance would be of great value to the boy.
Ma Tante ran this tiny business single-handed. The kitchen
was just behind the shop.

I had made no profound study of this background, which
came bit by bit to life. My own acquaintance with the older
parts of Paris in the days when the police still wore the long
cape and the bicycling *hirondelles* patrolled the streets. I had
read much early Simenon: as a young reporter he had met

the famous Xavier Guichard, Director of the first real PJ; had known the legendary medical examiner, Doctor Paul (a year ago *Poulet Docteur* was still on the menu at Lapérouse, and maybe still is). But the 'crystallization' – Stendhal's famous metaphor of the branch left in the salt-mine – was my admiration of a wonderful actor, Louis Jouvet, and his extraordinary composition of the old police officer in *Quai des Orfèvres*.

The police was (and still is) very much a law unto itself. The commissariats and police-posts were dreadful rats' nests belonging to the early nineteenth century; the basements under the Palais de Justice were and still are medieval, of horrible squalor. Old people still spoke of the *sergents-de-ville*, moustached veterans, generally drunk, whose outward bonhomie could turn very suddenly to extreme brutality. Supposedly, the upper ranks had been purged at the Liberation. In reality most of the collaborators under the Vichy regime survived untouched but a great many turpitudes got swept under the carpet; archives vanished or were simply inaccessible and lips stayed sealed. When I spoke of these matters in private conversation with a young, modern PJ Commissaire he grinned. Better not to ask; you won't get anywhere with indiscreet questions – amused by my naïveté. 'Richard', in later years a Divisional Commissaire and Castang's chief, was a survival from these times. He knew a great many secrets.

Corruption was universal. In the upper reaches, grave criminal charges could be and were watered down to nothing. Effaced. Shelved, and forgotten, buried under reams of dilatory procedure. 'Knowing somebody' of influence in politics or the administration was the key; a word in the right ear was enough. At the lower end, misdemeanours and even felonies were dealt with by popping in for a quiet word and a bribe to the station 'brigadier'. In a room full of resting policemen the phrase *Je paye l'apéro* was often enough. The waiter from the pub next door came in with a bottle of pastis, and parking tickets were torn up. Indeed it is all to be found in Simenon. Maigret himself is suspended from duty under a cloud, because the abortionist dentist is friendly with a Minister. While on the day-by-day level, the boozing in the Brasserie Dauphine, the 'local' of the Quai des Orfèvres, was something chronic ... The foreigner, who thought that the Scotland Yard Inspector was the answer to everything, got confused among the intricate bureaucracies of the 'parallel police'. What on earth was the 'Sureté' in the rue des Saussaies, under the eye and thumb of the Minister of the Interior? What was 'Renseignements Généraux' which belongs to the Premier Ministre? Who accounts for the secret funds? What indeed are the exact attributions of the Prefect of Police? Even the regional services of the Police Judiciaire had not been invented in Castang's early days on the streets of Paris.

The picture was perfunctory. I could feel sure that he lacked confidence, was uncertain of his own identity, needed what we would now call structure in his world, wanted to give loyalty and obedience to a hierarchy, wished to 'belong', was happy under orders and comfortable wearing a uniform. He would feel stable and would be quick to reach out for responsibility. He would not be left for long on patrol duty. Few of the rank and file had intelligence, fewer still could see – or wanted to see – further than a yard beyond their face, while a boy with a university degree was then a rarity. Get him out of that and send him to officer-schooling.

The experience was valuable. He learned cold and wet, hardihood and patience, how to stand still and how to run, how to take knocks and when to give them. That the poor are always oppressed, and the rich never, he knew already, but that justice is a legal fiction, that night duty is a different world – there were a lot of lessons he would not forget. The most valuable beyond doubt was how to block emotion. The police world is filth and abominable smells; brutality, cruelty and insanity. By immovable tradition, the population of Paris hates and distrusts the police, admires and respects the fire brigade, is docile and even humble before the emergency-ward nurse, spits in the eye of sympathy. Being unsentimental, without becoming totally anaesthetized, is never all that easy. He had been a uniformed cop. A good thing for an officer to remember.

There were a lot of changes around this time, many of them cosmetic in the tiresome French way of calling the same thing by new names; when these are ponderous they use the acronym. The former junior inspector began to be known as an *officier de police adjoint*, so that one spoke of an OPA. The most important and far-reaching of these reforms was the creation of the Regional Services. Every large city had its own, with authority over the corresponding province. The SRPJ became at once an elaborate bureaucracy with its specialized brigades and subgroups, in conflict with the gendarmerie, the traditional authority in rural areas. The gendarmerie is military – comes under the Ministry of Defence – which makes things worse. There is also friction with the local municipal police. Overlapping responsibilities take up a vast amount of time and trouble, need a great deal of tact if things are to run smoothly. They never do.

The Regional Service is headed by a Divisional Commissaire, who lives in hopes of promotion to a plum posting (Versailles is the summit; above this are only the half-dozen superjobs like Controller and General Inspector) while living in terror of banishment to some hell-hole. Under him are some group heads, middle- and junior-grade commissaires; a chief of staff is needed and Castang was good at this. Commissaires-school is at St Cyr du Mont d'Or, just outside Lyon. I asked them once what proportion of women they thought suitable. 'Five per cent.' Nothing more macho than the police. In the Magistrates school at Bordeaux the figure is up to seventy.

Castang felt dislike for these strongholds of reaction. He picked women colleagues whenever he could and got on well with them. Of course this was twenty years ago. 'In men's circles, where cowardice is the first rule of social intercourse, straight talking is contrary to prevailing etiquette.' That is the formidable Martine Aubry speaking: Castang, wherever he is, would smile.

It is comic now to find myself looking at him with this impersonal eye, a total detachment. Those many years we lived and worked together, so that at the end of the day the one would say 'Time for a beer' to the other. There are eighteen of these books and I have no opinion about their merit; never reread them and don't intend to and am now vague about their content; I can certainly not recall the various intrigues and turns of narrative. Across the years, enough people have told me they have value for me to believe it. It would be natural for them to vary much in quality. I feel now a sorrow that they did not do better with the public. There were always enthusiasms, and in some countries much warm and real praise. It was easy enough to see why in France they were always refused, with something like horror. In England they had an ambiguous and generally half-hearted welcome. Reviewers are a poor lot at best; their masters, the literary editors, undistinguished. I feel no interest in raking over these ashes.

Luck exists. There is in this world an arbitrary factor of chance unaccountable by any means known to us. There are skilled hard-headed gamblers who are clever at calculating odds, and there is the wayward arrow of the Lotto win, and there are also people we know who seem consistently favoured by the smile of fortune. An equal number – one must presume – are visited by misfortune more often that appears normal. We cannot help speculating. I have often done so, since I have as often thought myself consistently unlucky, but these marks of chagrin stay in the memory, while amazing strokes of good luck glide past, our vanity claiming them as no more than our due: they may never be noticed at all. For we say 'Oh, bad luck' of the man in the road accident (he was not drunk or even imprudent; it just hit him...) but only a dramatic hair's breadth escape would be called lucky; the others in front or behind were not noticed. However, in the genes and in the temperament there is a bent; it is given us and we do our best with it.

Looking back upon my life, I see astonishing foolishness, the most reckless irresponsibility, such flagrant bad judgement that I cannot forgive, that the good fortune seems really to outweigh the bad. One factor only, which has always been mine, woven in from the start, has been beyond my power to alter: the lack of energy. This as I believe is the real reason why my work did not have more success. One can see it in paintings; the best possess an energy which the second-rate, however imaginative and craftsmanly, never quite reaches. It is physical: a merely nervous energy is not enough. I am quite a good writer, but of these the world has plenty. One will say afterwards that one was lazy, bored or indifferent, but the truth was plain exhaustion.

To be 'someone things happen to'; is that an aspect of chance? Of character, rather. I do not care greatly for Conrad's *Chance* (it was my father's favourite book, which tells one something about him); I find Marlow's unstoppable garrulity and knowingness tedious. But after the blackest horrors Captain Anthony, a good man, 'happens' to poor battered Flora de Barral – and so will young Powell. Vera happens to Castang and it is the most interesting thing that could or would. He is ordinary; a civil-service functionary of average intelligence enlivened by a spark or two of humour; honest and conscientious at a not very demanding job. He would be noted by his superiors as a good second, if strongly led; capable and industrious, if inclined to be lazy. Pleasant chap, liked by his colleagues; now and again awkward. Won't reach heights, and forty years from now will take the pension due to a competent seniority and experience.

The wife changed all this. Meeting her was 'chance'? The

little Czech girl wanted to run away to the glorious West; being a gymnast gave her an opening, but she didn't know how. The sulking girl would simply be caught, disciplined, sent home in disgrace. But the police officer on crowd duty at the competition took her under his wing and to give her refugee status married her. It happened in reality quite often; my uncle Mike, a notable boy-lover, made a *mariage blanc* for the same reason, followed by a quickie divorce. But to Castang marrying was serious: his own past imposed that. This kind of impulse did his career no good at all. Vera feeling pitied and hating it – not the best way to start a marriage. A strong character, and not merely obstinate, she determined not to be outdone in generosity. The accident which left her legs semi-paralysed for a year or more was, I think, something more than chance. But I am not a fount of wisdom – as is Marlow.

She brought ideals with her and the strong principles of her father, an Old-Communist and a railwayman, of a type once frequent in France, who believed that a public service demanded the best of oneself and to whom slackness on the job was anathema. She had certainly no grievance at the severe discipline imposed on the girls in the gymnastic team: her hatreds were for nepotism, corruption and hypocrisy. She was lonely and often unhappy in France and found it difficult to make friends; lived much driven in upon herself. Her influence upon Castang's character was great. There was always a good deal he could not tell her. As he climbed in rank and responsibility the stiffness of her moral joints got easier but she would remain uncompromising upon a question of honour. Some concepts did not go out of date. People respected this, Castang most of all, whatever his failures. She taught him to loathe violence and to despise vengeance.

It was thus impossible for him to exist in the context of conventional crime fiction, in which the extremes of violence are the daily commonplace, and to seek revenge the natural emotional reaction. It was inevitable, indeed, that these books should be actively disliked by many.

Towards the end of my own life I am unrepentant. The price to pay has been considerable and I have complained a lot – as also Castang did, pretty often.

7

GREEN SWANS, WHITE SWANS

WHEN THE CHILDREN WERE SMALL we had a record of traditional folklore songs by a Dutch children's choir. These are very similar to the English equivalents; settings for the steps and movements of street games often some hundreds of years old. Rhythmed for a skipping-rope or the chalked squares of *la marelle* – women are the guardians of the collective memory but the little girls did not hesitate to distort words or names they did not understand.

> *Groene Zwanen, Witte Zwanen,*
> *Wie gaat er mee naar Engeland varen?*

Who goes along, sailing to England? Is this some echo of the Sea War in Charles II's time, blood-stained but after several battles indecisive: moral victory went to the Dutch after their bold raid up the Medway, capturing the *Royal Charles* and causing fearful havoc? (Mr Pepys was frightened into burying all his money under an apple tree; later furious since nobody could remember which one, and they had to dig up the whole garden at dead of night.) Were the swans on somebody's coat of arms? What is their significance, the kinship to 'Oranges and Lemons'?

For the rhyme gets dark. England is tight shut. The key has been lost. In all the land there is no smith who knows how to forge it. The Dutch knew well that English harbours and the prevailing winds would always lock the sea approaches; they could not win a prolonged war. Thereafter, indeed, they would always seek alliance with England, against the greater menace of France, and this thinking has persisted to our own days. Mr Pepys loved and respected Holland, greatly envied their superior administration, but foresaw his Navy's might and mastery.

The rhyme has for me a special echo. I would sail many times to and fro across the North Sea. I would live still and work, for some years, in England. But I had lost the key and would never again know how to forge it.

The year was 1951, the affair simple, a possible job in a hotel kitchen, which came to nothing and my stay was no more than a week. But I knew, I think, from the first glimpse of a Dutch town: Maassluis, the boat-train to Amsterdam stops there a moment. Early on a raw morning all the windows were open and the bed-linen put out to air. One would not see that in England. Coming out of the Central Station in Amsterdam a million seagulls hung talking angrily in the unmistakable local accent; the Prins Hendrikkade was bathed in blazing sun but this scarcely seemed to alter the 'painters' light'. It took possession. I do not believe in past lives which – it is said – can sometimes cast shadows into the present, waking atavistic recollections. But I knew I had come home.

In these immediate post-war years Holland was a dour place, still downtrodden among bitter memories of the Occupation, of the hungry winter of 1944, of uniformed Gestapo men in the Euterpestraat. 'There were two sorts of police, the black which were theirs and the green which were ours. Ours were the worse.' An English face and voice was kindly seen and made welcome; these had careered across the country in tank and troop-carrier on the way up to Arnhem. We were still the Liberators for whom bells had rung and the people had waved flags and cheered: most of them anyhow. There were no tourists then. A fraternal feeling predominated; England too was poor now and the Empire was on the way out. The tremendous Dutch empire of Insulinde was gone already, amid much emotion: a singularly hard-headed lot, the Dutch, but few were delighted, really, to be rid of it. People were busy – it is a hard-working folk – making a new and a modern Holland, since the old one had so singularly failed, but the sights and sounds and smells were still those of the pre-war Kingdom of the Netherlands, a fiercely tight-knit and self-contained corner of Europe. 'Holland is a very small family, Meneer,' a policeman would tell me ten years later. My love was given open and complete.

Here I found a wife. On that children's record, 'Next Door the Green Swans' was the one about the little girl who is out too late. *'Amsterdamse Meisje, wat doe jij hier zo laat op straat?'*[7] Her answer is sung solo, a thin child's soprano. 'I am going for my little sister, who is still at our auntie's house. She would be frightened alone, in the twilight.' I can pin-point the moment; I too had been out all day; had arranged to pick her up in the café of the Central Station; arrived at last rather late: surely she would have gone home? She was at a table alone with a cup of cold coffee, sitting very upright, staring at the wall opposite, oblivious to the man in the doorway who stopped to take a photo and store it away in his mind. One does not always know the exact moment of falling in love. One will also take pains to avoid sentimentalizing. She was the sister of a friend, had been showing me the kindness of translating when needed; I knew no Dutch then. Like all northern countries with obscure languages Holland is quick to drop into English, but there were and are plenty of people who can't and I was grateful for her help. I would take much pains to learn a correct, polite, academic Dutch. It can sound awful, with a great many lazy elisions and a dreadful nasal whine. Her own was unusually pure, free of the trailing Amsterdam accent: they are snobbish here about the rest of Holland, which appears to them comically provincial. When we married the following year in the then-pleasant town of Brighton, which she came much to love, she would talk English to me and I would talk to her in my new-found Dutch, which pleased her.

---

7. 'Little Amsterdam girl, what are you doing out so late on the street?'

The time came, a time of great happiness, when we would live in Holland together. My two eldest children gave me the proof of the flexibility they all have when small enough, going from an English school to a Dutch one and within a short while a French school, without being in the least traumatized.

Why not stay put? Others asked and so have I. The immediate pretexts, as with leaving England, were flimsy. More to the point, why not go back? The schools in Strasbourg, the university – yes, yes, of good quality. The European ideal – it was then remote and largely theoretical. True, the ancient Rhineland civilization is here alive, has never altogether petered out even at the height of nationalist fervour. Dürer came to study here, and Goethe. People read and speak German here as readily as French. The distance to Prague or to Cracow is no greater than to Paris. The crossroads city stood always upon the east-west axis of Europe, and also that from north to south; the painters' road. North still of the Alps but here one feels the breath of the south (as one does in Munich).

It was Vera who gave me the true answer. She was not 'my wife', as journalists have crudely supposed. The writer lifts from half a dozen sources: as many of the vivid and talkative women in the Faubourg Saint Germain of Proust's day went into Oriane de Guermantes. Vera indeed bears no resemblance to my wife, but the two women had one trait in common: the one's 'Czechness' grew out of the other's 'Dutchness'.

I see no need to make a fuss; I have known too many psychiatrists, and when Nabokov gives way to his lifelong distaste for 'the Viennese quack' one can often feel oneself on his side. It is enough to say that my wife in adolescence suffered an enormous injustice, for which the State was responsible. She did not – does not – wish to pass her life within that tight little family. One can be more freely and more truly Dutch outside those damnable frontiers: this is among the metaphysical bonds between us. She felt – much like Vera – little sympathy for the Frenchness of France: both women made the most of it, grumbling a good deal. Speaking German freely she acquired a tolerance for Strasbourg. But to live in Amsterdam? No – and no reason is offered.

Make a right pair, don't they. More than a bit there of the blind leading the paralysed, ending in a dorp nobody has heard of, nor would ever want to. It seemed easier to write about the village when we were ready to leave tomorrow. Piles of old junk; let the children take whatever they want and throw the rest away. Nobody will much want a house like this; too big and too awkward: selling it will pay for a move, anyhow. People won't bother with the garden – beyond wondering what possessed me. Plenty of much better space on the far side, assuming an enthusiasm. It would be good enough for a young couple, all this, with a few children; much what we were ourselves those many years ago: there are still people with children. One could do a great deal worse. The village has kept its school, and the little shop, and the butcher makes his round. Indeed it is now a young village, active and prosperous. Down the road in Schirmeck the railway still runs; people think nothing of going to work in the city.

As for ourselves, seventy is no age. Is it going to be Berlin or Barcelona? Everyone has noticed how simple and rapid it is now; boys, girls of seventeen studying in Toulouse or Milano run home for the weekend. As I write these words a child of ours – good god he's forty – is on holiday in New Mexico; not expensive, they borrowed a caravan from a friend. Would for us have been an extraordinary adventure and they make nothing of it.

Humour will be a help. Aged seventy, barely three years ago, I acquired illnesses of startling banality ('everyone's got it, it's this year's fashion') as well as things I had never heard of and which amused doctors. 'Whenever I see Mr Freeling he has thought of something original.' Within the space of a twelvemonth, a day in Strasbourg would be as much effort as a trip to Valparaiso; to walk, here on my familiar hills, as harsh as to climb Annapurna.

Frank Churchill went to London to have his hair cut: the village disapproved and Mr Knightley thought it showed a bad disposition. But one cannot be ruled, inspired or even guided by Jane. It would be as foolish to imitate notable globetrotters like Dickens or Stevenson. To be sure, Stendhal pottered all over Europe, alert to beauty and the ridiculous; it nourished his spirit. Paris and London were, and are, impossibly provincial, blinded by self-importance and cronyism; one cannot behave as though they do not exist. If my feet are tied to Grandfontaine I am no longer a novelist.

To travel now that it is so dull is to invite boredom? 'Call me next time you're in LA and we'll lunch' said the studio head; an unusually deadening prospect of a sandwich and a monologue in his office. I was anyhow forever out of joint; nostalgic about pre-1914 trains (a sad day when they put an end to the Dover-Dunkerque night ferry). A chronic lack, I have said already, of physical energies; the novelist's strength is in the nape of the neck. Stamina: a judge guffawed in court at a phrase of mine. Can't appear, sorry; being pushed along the front at Biarritz in a bath chair. I was being literary, but very nearly literal. Never could manage late nights, rooms full of people, parties ... My favourite meal is always like the old haircut-cliché, 'in silence'. None of this will do for a writer; these habits invite neglect, and at last contempt. Really it was no surprise, being struck down. Home is the hunter here in Grandfontaine.

Together with a little wad of manuscript – copies made of American poems first discovered, aged fifteen – was something which didn't belong; a yellowed sheet of English prose, which I must have come across, liked and wished to copy. I think it must be Robert Burton: it has that ornate, heavy-jointed feel. This is a happy find, and now that I am finished I propose to reproduce it here. The sheet is a scribble looking as though made on a bus; what could I have been doing? I can't guarantee the spelling, but they were very casual about this at the period. Even some of the wording (blame the bus). The surprise to me is only that at this age I had no conscious idea of becoming a writer. Fifty years later I am content to let it stand as I found it, folded in to 'Rhapsody on a Windy Night'.

Others at the Porches and entries of their Buildings set their Armes; I, my Picture; if any colours can deliver a minde so plaine, and flat, and through light as mine. Naturally at a new Author, I doubt, and sticke, and do not say quickly, good. I censure much, and taxe; and this liberty costs mee more than others, by how much my owne things are worse than others. Yet I would not be so rebellious against my selfe, as not to doe it, since I love it; nor so unjust to others, to do it [here are three illegible words which I cannot supply]. As long as I give them as good hold upon me, they must pardon me my bitinge. I forbid no reprehender, but him that like the Trent Councell forbids not bookes but Authors, damning whatever such a name hath or shall write. None writes so ill, that he gives not some thing exemplary, to follow, or flie. Now when I beginne this booke, I have no purpose to come into any man's debt; how my stocke will hold out I know not; perchance waste, perchance increase; if I doe borrow any thing of Antiquitie, besides that I make account that I pay it to Posterity, with as much and as good: you shall finde mee to acknowledge it, and to thanke not him only that hath digged out treasure for mee, but hath lighted mee a candle to the place.

And as at fifteen years old, so as seventy-five.

It is the end of October, a time I love above others. Rather a sad time in Grandfontaine; the crook of the road and the swell of the hill have cut the sunlight in half, and the house, in this narrow cranky dale, will have to look at the northern slope brilliant with the fall colours; itself shadowed and diminished. Many years ago I had this ground cleared of sombre evergreens. Plantations of gaiety and light replaced them and these will illuminate the new century which is not mine.

This last autumn of our dying twentieth is sunlit as few have been over these hundred years. The vintage is of unusual promise and in Champagne they are counting, greedily and gleefully, the heaped-up piles of louis-d'or. Full of youth and hope, my parents came thrusting into a new century; I have grandchildren the same age. Perhaps, in the year 2027, a child will be born, as I was. That child will know nothing of me, will be uninterested. Some faded old aunt might have spoken of me, remembering perhaps a joke made when she was herself a little girl. 'Sometimes he made us laugh.' There is a minute possibility that this child may come across this book; turn a page or two wondering what all that was about, and – who knows? – break into laughter.